Schöningh

TEACHERS' BOOK

Discover ...

TOPICS FOR ADVANCED LEARNERS

edited by Engelbert Thaler

The Media

From Printing to Podcasts

by Stephen Speight and Karsten Witsch

www.schoeningh-schulbuch.de
Schöningh Verlag, Jühenplatz 1–3, 33098 Paderborn

Druck 5 4 3 2 1 / Jahr 2014 13 12 11 10
Die letzte Zahl bezeichnet das Jahr dieses Druckes.

Umschlaggestaltung: Franz-Josef Domke, Hannover
Umschlagabbildung: © Rainer F. Steussloff/Intro
Druck und Bindung: Media-Print Informationstechnologie GmbH, Paderborn

ISBN 978-3-14-040121-0

Inhaltsverzeichnis

Die didaktische Konzeption

Die Themenheftreihe *Discover* ... richtet sich an Schülerinnen und Schüler der Sekundarstufe II und bereitet in Anlehnung an die Einheitlichen Prüfungsanforderungen in der Abiturprüfung (EPA) und die Rahmenrichtlinien der einzelnen Bundesländer interkulturell relevante, Jugendliche interessierende Themen methodisch-didaktisch auf.

Der Einstieg in das Thema, das in mehrere Kapitel untergliedert ist, erfolgt über eine Doppelseite „Getting started“ mit Bildmaterial und einigen Einstiegsaufgaben. Die Texte weisen unterschiedliche Längen auf, sind aber insgesamt nicht zu lang und berücksichtigen verschiedene Textsorten. Reichlich Bildmaterial (Fotos, Zeichnungen, Cartoons, Grafiken, Tabellen, Karten etc.) ist funktional in die Texte und Aufgabenapparate integriert.

Der Aufbau der einzelnen Texte ermöglicht einen klar strukturierten Unterricht mit drei Phasen: *pre*, *while* und *post reading*. *Pre-reading*-Aufgaben führen zum Text hin, rufen das Vorwissen ab und bauen Erwartungshaltungen auf. Der eigentliche Leseprozess wird im Sinne eines *guided reading* durch gelegentliche Lesebeobachtungsaufgaben und (sparsame) Annotationen in den Fußnoten unterstützt. Im abschließenden Aufgabenapparat unter dem Titel „Activities“ werden alle Fragen zu thematisch zusammengehörigen Blöcken mit einer kurzen inhaltlichen Überschrift in der Randspalte zusammengefasst. Diese Aufgaben lassen sich den drei maßgeblichen Bereichen zuordnen:
a) Inhalt (*comprehension*)
b) Struktur, Intention, Stil, Sprache (*analysis*)
c) Evaluation, eigene Meinungsäußerung, sprachproduktive kreative Aufgaben (*evaluation and creation*).

Prof. Dr. Engelbert Thaler, Herausgeber

Discover ... The Media – From Printing to Podcasts

Tabellarische Textübersicht

About the Mass Media – Something for Everyone

Autor, Text	Inhaltliche Schwerpunkte	Textsorte	Wortzahl ca.
A Great life?	Comparison between the 'good old days' and the present day in media terms	Argumentative text	180
Yevgeny Zamyatin: WE	Zamyatin describes a world under a dictator called 'The Benefactor', where imagination is regarded as a weakness because it prevents people from being as 'perfect' as machines	fictional text from a dystopian novel	370
Alice Fisher: Celebrity Etiquette	Semi-humorous text about the way celebrity mothers exploit their babies	Column from a colour supple-ment of a Sunday newspa-per	250
Karen Ross and Virginia Nightingale: When Information Rules	The text deals with the way the once passive audience for one medium at a time has become an active, participating audience with access to many different media.	Extract from an academic textbook	320
Worksheet im Lehrerheft			
Worksheet 1, S. 16	George Orwell: Big Brother Is Watching *You*!		

Newspapers and Teenage Magazines – The Shocking Truth

Autor, Text	Inhaltliche Schwerpunkte	Textsorte	Wortzahl ca.
Front Pages	Memorable front pages from a range of newspapers	Newspaper headlines and photographs	–
Nick Cohen: Press Freedom	Attitudes to press freedom in east and west	Newspaper column	380
Evelyn Waugh: Scoop	Humorous/satirical views of the popular press's attitude to news/the truth	Extracts from a satirical novel	190 + 210
Amanda Cable: Not What Daddy Had in Mind!	Well-educated English girl falls for and marries African. Goes to live with him in Tanzania in relative poverty.	Newspaper article from a semi-popular newspaper	1770
Magazines for Teenagers	Summaries of the contents of typical magazines bought by teenage boys and girls respectively	Information in tabular form	–
Worksheet im Lehrerheft			
Worksheet 2, S. 32	Writing a News Story		

Advertising – Buy One, Get One Free

Autor, Text	Inhaltliche Schwerpunkte	Textsorte	Wortzahl ca.
Where to Begin?	Information summary dealing with characters used by advertisers and the psychological weaknesses which the advertisers exploit	Brief information via graphics and text	140
Onward Christian Admen	A local council wishes to treat a cross outside a church as an advertisement	Humorous leading article	170
Sarah-Kate Templeton: 'Misleading' Winston Milk Ads Pulled	A leading scientist and television presenter is taken to task for appearing in questionable commercials for milk which it is claimed will make children do better in school	Investigative journalism	660
James Mills: Pencil Case With a Playboy Bunny Logo Is Banned by School	A little girl did not realise that the Playboy logo on her new pencil case had anything to do with soft pornography – until her school complained	Newspaper article	230
Upgrade-itis	Illustrated series of short articles pointing out how rapidly electronic equipment becomes out of date	Survey article	460
Nick Christian: Power Pestering Costs Parents a Cool £3bn	Pressure exerted by children on parents to buy desirable items	Short comment	140
Cuttings	Short extracts dealing with a number of advertising-related topics	Short extracts from newspaper articles	1020
When Don't Smoke Means Do	Critical article pointing out that campaigns by tobacco companies which appear to be trying to stop young people smoking may actually have the opposite effect	Investigative journalism	430
And Finally ...	Montage of large, striking advertisements	Typical, mainly visual advertisements	–
Worksheet im Lehrerheft			
Worksheet 3, S. 47	Harwich to Hook		

Computers and the Internet – Whatever Next?

Autor, Text	Inhaltliche Schwerpunkte	Textsorte	Wortzahl ca.
Plug in and Play	Introductory material including visual material (a man surrounded by electronic devices) and a selection of key terms for the topic	Brief introduction to the topic	–
Jonathan D. Glater: Cheaters at College Shift to Higher Tech	The article deals with modern methods of cheating, and attempts by college staff to prevent students from using them	Newspaper article	670
Stephen King: Will We Close the Book on Books?	A 'hymn of praise' in favour of books old and new now that they are under threat from new media	Personal statement on the Internet	270
David Smith: The Next Big Thing	Current and future developments on the internet	Brief informational text	200
Janet Kornblum: Campuses Connect Students Online	Description of non-official websites at universities and students' favourable response to them	Newspaper article	600
Rob Waugh: The World Is Not Enough	Dramatic description of virtual reality on the 'Second World' website	Feature article from a colour supplement	490
Worksheet im Lehrerheft			
Worksheet 4, S. 60	A Survey		

Films and TV – Wide Screens for Narrow Minds?

Autor, Text	Inhaltliche Schwerpunkte	Textsorte	Wortzahl ca.
Cartoons	The cartoons make a series of mainly negative comments about television	Cartoons	–
Neil Postman: Amusing Ourselves to Death	Postman claims that television has turned all kinds of human experience into entertainment	Argumentative text: extract from a nonfiction book	340
Green Day: I Want to Be on TV	The song deals with the 'attractions' of being on TV and becoming a celebrity	Satirical song text	99
Bruce Springsteen: 57 Channels (And Nothin' On)	The singer makes heroic efforts to get some worthwhile entertainment from his TV, but fails, so his girlfriend leaves, and he blows up the set with a .44 Magnum	Satirical song text	260
Pink: Stupid Girls	The song deals with the disastrous consequences (for girls) of aping minor celebrities in the hope of joining them	Protest song	410
Ben Macintyre: Coming Soon, the End of a Cinema Near You?	The author claims that the cinema experience is unique, and will survive in spite of all the alternative ways of watching films which are now available	Newspaper column	430
Worksheet im Lehrerheft			
Worksheet 5, S. 73	Vocabulary – Talking about the Media		

Steam Radio – Still a 'Hot' Medium?

Autor, Text	Inhaltliche Schwerpunkte	Textsorte	Wortzahl ca.
What's on the Radio Today?/Time to Tune in	Role of radio past and present, plus an overview of a typical day's BBC radio programmes	Informational texts	–
Stephen Fry: Hallo!	Historical origins and uses of 'Hallo' as an exclamation and greeting	Transcript of a radio feature	1500

Yesterday's Tomorrows – Future Imperfect?

Autor, Text	Inhaltliche Schwerpunkte	Textsorte	Wortzahl ca.
Ray Bradbury: The Veldt	The dangers of virtual reality when it becomes too real	Short story (science fiction)	4600
Ray Bradbury: The Murderer	One man rebels against a world where there is no escape from a continual barrage of sounds of all kinds	Short story (science fiction)	2800
Worksheets und Klausuren im Lehrerheft			
Worksheet 6, S. 92	A Puzzle Page – Part I		
Worksheet 7, S. 94	A Puzzle Page – Part II		
Klausur 1, S. 97	Morton Rhue, Give a Boy a Gun		
Klausur 1, S. 99	Daniel Frampton, Moving Images		

Getting started

Unterrichtsempfehlungen

Die Hinführung durch den Abschnitt „Getting started" leistet einen sehr guten Einstieg in das Thema des Schülerbuches und eignet sich zum Aufbau von Zielspannung. Motivierend und Neugier erweckend erscheint diese Hinführung besonders deshalb, da sie vielfach an die Interessen der Lernenden anknüpft. Der Themenkreis „Mittelalter" (u.a. historische, mittelalterliche Romane, Verfilmungen wie „Das Parfum"), erfreut sich bei den Schülerinnen und Schülern großer Beliebtheit.

Solutions

Activities p. 4

What kind of person do you think this was?
He was unworldly, unsuccessful in his 'job', poor, probably didn't have much of a sense of humour, very much the academic type.

What did Chaucer think of him?
Chaucer obviously didn't exactly warm to him, but had a certain respect for his love of books and ascetic way of life.

What language had the bible been in until then?
Latin

Was it originally written in that language?
No. Original versions, where they exist, are in Aramaic.

Activities p. 5

Name some people who you think deserve to be famous – and some who don't.
Personal choices. The so-called 'celebrity cult' is likely to come up, plus the relative merits/salaries of politicians, footballers, top business people, pop musicians etc.

About the Mass Media – Something for Everyone

Vorbemerkung zum Kapitel

Mit dem ersten Kapitel wird eine Brücke in unsere Zeit geschlagen. Ganz im Sinne des Titels des Kapitels wird hier die Relevanz und Präsenz neuer Medien für unser/in unserem Leben beleuchtet. Dabei werden die sich aus dem Umgang mit Medien und Informationstechnologien ergebenden positiven wie negativen Konsequenzen kritisch beleuchtet.

A Great Life?

Text and photos

A brief introduction to the topic, comparing our media/information/travel dominated world with (agricultural) life in the past. The cartoons provide humorous comments on and illustrations of some of the points made.

Synopsis

Before the mass media people could live in privacy, but they had very little access to entertainment of any kind, and the great majority did not travel much either. We, on the other hand, have data stored about us in all kinds of places, but we have access to vast amounts of entertainment, and can travel cheaply to other parts of the world.

Unterrichtsempfehlungen

Der Impuls „Name some people ...“ (Schülerbuch S. 5) sollte aufgegriffen werden und zur Einführung des ersten Kapitels – insbesondere des Cartoons auf der linken Seite – funktional genutzt werden. Die ersten zwei Aufgaben des Aufgabenapparates können in Gruppenarbeit bearbeitet werden. Im Sinne der Philosophie des Kooperativen Lernens und der Phasierung *Think – Pair – Share*, sollten die Lernenden das Ziel anvisieren, zu einem gemeinsamen, stichhaltigen Präsentationsergebnis zu gelangen. Abstrahierend müssen die zentralen Punkte aus den Präsentationen von der Lehrerin/dem Lehrer gebündelt werden – abhängig von der Leistungsstärke des Kurses entweder in Form eines kurzen Lehrervortrags oder eines Tafelanschriebs.
Die dritte Aufgabe ist schriftlich zu bearbeiten; die Aufgabenstellung stellt im Hinblick auf das Zentralabitur eine geeignete Übung dar.

Solutions

Activities p. 6

1. **Make brief notes on the content of the text, giving each point a rating (+, – or ?) and indicating whether the author is referring to the past or the present.**
   - No photographs/newspapers (–) past
   - No surveillance systems (+) past
   - Boring evenings after tiring work (–) past
   - Very little travel (–) past
   - Personal data stored in many places (–) present
   - Assaulted by a flood of words and images (–) present
   - Huge amount of entertainment of all kinds available (+) present
   - Cheap holiday flights (+) present

   The last two points could also be seen as partly negative – the quality of entertainment available is often poor, and cheap flights are bad from an environmental point of view.

2. **How far do you agree with his assessment?**
   – students will probably feel that this is a reasonable view
   – seen largely in black and white terms in the interests of brevity
   – deliberately a bit provocative

3. **What annoys you about modern life? Are there any aspects of life in the past which you think you would have enjoyed?**
   Points which could be made:
   – too much traffic/pollution, etc.
   – life generally hectic, exam pressures for students
   – the celebrity cult – people famous just for being famous
   – persistence of poverty in rich countries as well as poor
   – problems with some aspects of modern life, e. g. call centres, delays at airports, computers
   – poor quality of much TV
   – the aristocracy had a good life in the past
   – some people think village life was attractive in the past (others would disagree – power of the church – disapproval of sex before marriage etc.)

WE

Yevgeny Zamyatin

Text This short extract is a dramatic description of efforts in a dystopian society to stamp out the 'inconvenient' characteristic of the human imagination, which interferes with the smooth running of society. Zamyatin piles on the propaganda for the operation which will achieve this, leaving the reader to think about the positive consequences of possessing imagination – and the terrible consequences of losing it.

Synopsis The text consists of a fictional article from the official newspaper of the One State. It explains that until now machines have been more perfect than human beings, although humans have become quite good at working in time with machines. The one remaining problem is the imagination, which the One State sees as a disease which makes people unhappy and unreliable. Now that State Science has located the seat of the imagination in the brain, everyone is invited to hurry along to have their imagination removed by X-ray cauterizing so that they can become perfect and perfectly happy.

Unterrichtsempfehlungen

Als Einstieg lohnt eine Beschreibung des vorstehenden Bildmaterials. Zunächst sollte im Sinne von Bildbeschreibungstechniken das Abgebildete verbalisiert werden. Besonders leistungsschwächere oder in der mündlichen Mitarbeit zurückhaltende Schülerinnen und Schüler lassen sich hier gut aktivieren. Im Anschluss kann das Plenum das Beschriebene in Verbindung setzen zu den Begriffen „utopia“ bzw. „dystopia“.
Dem Vorwissen der Lernenden ist dabei Rechnung zu tragen. Sollten die Begriffe völlig unbekannt sein, muss vor der Bearbeitung der Bilder und des Textes eine Klärung vorgenommen werden. Dies kann durch einen prägnanten Lehrervortrag oder aber durch die Bearbeitung von überschaubarem Zusatzmaterial, das die Lehrkraft bereitstellt, erfolgen. In jedem Fall ist ein Verständnis der Begriffe „utopia“ und „dystopia“ im Hinblick auf das Zentralabitur unumgänglich. Ferner ergibt sich auch nur so eine ertragreiche Beantwortung der Aufgaben 3 und 4 der Activities. Das Ergebnis der pre-reading-Aufgabe kann an der Tafel zusammengefasst werden:

Some typical features of dystopias:

- a dictator/big brother figure
- people have no freedom
- sinister methods used to ensure conformity
- "doublethink" – people expected to believe good news all the time although their situation is actually miserable
- secret police in some form
- indoctrination/brainwashing attempts to change human nature permanently

Die Aufgaben 1 und 2 führen zu einem sicheren und differenzierten Textverständnis. Die Lernenden könnten dazu motiviert werden, die Aufgaben in Partnerarbeit zu lösen und ihre Antworten in eine bildliche/grafische Form („What is ‚wrong' ..." – „cure") zu präsentieren. Die Präsentation kann in Form eines kurzen Museumsgangs erfolgen. Ein inhaltlich und sprachlich gesichertes Ergebnis sollte von der Lehrkraft mit dem Plenum dann an der Tafel abstrahiert werden. Der Museumsgang kann hier u. a. auch als Fördermaßnahme bzw. Entlastung verstanden werden, der besonders schwächeren und auch schüchternen Lernern Sicherheit vermittelt, um sich aktiv in der Phase der Bündelung und Zusammenführung zentraler, tragfähiger Aspekte zu beteiligen. In sehr leistungsstarken Lerngruppen sind alternative Prozesse zu erwägen. Zur Bearbeitung der 3. Aufgabe sollten die Schülerinnen und Schüler die gesuchten Begriffe in Einzelarbeit unterstreichen und später als Grundlage für eine Diskussion im Plenum nutzen. Wichtige Aspekte sollten während der Diskussion von der Lehrerin/dem Lehrer notiert werden und am Ende in einem kurzen Lehrervortrag gebündelt werden. Die Aufgabe 4 fügt sich dann schlüssig als schriftliche Hausaufgabe an.
Die letzte Aufgabe (Nr. 5) regt zu handlungsorientierten/szenischen Umsetzungen an (z. B. eine in Gruppen vorbereitete Radio-/Fernsehansprache, ein Flugblatt, eine Rede, ein Verhör/Interview ...).
Abhängig von der Leistungsstärke eines Kurses sollte die Lehrkraft bis zu 3 Unterrichtsstunden für die vorstehend skizzierten Unterrichtsempfehlungen einplanen.

Solutions

Activities p. 9

1. **What is "wrong" with people according to the announcement in the *One State Gazette*?**
   Their imagination makes them less happy than machines, and less perfect in terms of the way they function.

2. **How can they be "cured"?**
   They can be cured by means of an operation which destroys the seat of the imagination, which State Science has located in the brain.

3. **What terms used in the text suggest that we are dealing with a non-democratic society?**
   One State, you shall be perfect, the Taylor system, the Guardians, State Science, cured of imagination, machine-like, the Great Operation, the Benefactor

4. **How do these terms clash with the style of the text? Why is it written in this way?**
   The style of the text suggests that the Great Operation will be a wonderful thing for everyone. It is pure propaganda intended to persuade everyone to have the operation, so that they will become "happy", docile and reliable like machines, which suits the One State's purposes.

5. **Assuming you could not be locked up or executed for arguing with an official in the One State, how would you go about defending the imagination as a valuable human faculty?**
   Points which could be made:
   – no art of any kind
   – no new discoveries in the sciences
   – no romantic love
   – no ability to appreciate the natural world
   – almost total loss of individuality

Celebrity Etiquette

Alice Fisher

Text and photographs

This short article from a Colour Supplement is a typical example of the celebrity culture. The (fairly) famous women in the photos are made fun of to some extent, but readers still want to know all about them.

Synopsis

Celebrity parents have a hard life. They can't always get as much money as they were hoping for for photos of their new baby. They are in competition with other celebrities to launch their own baby clothing brands, and they can come in for severe criticism for behaviour felt to be inappropriate for an ideal mum. We could feel sorry for them if they weren't making so much money and getting so much publicity.

Unterrichtsempfehlungen

Die Lektüre des Zeitungstextes kann als vorbereitende Hausaufgabe erfolgen oder aber zu Beginn einer Doppelstunde in Einzelarbeit erfolgen. Vokabular sollte nur in sehr leistungsschwachen Lerngruppen oder Kursen mit einer hohen Anzahl von „Seiteneinsteigern" bereitgestellt werden.
In der Unterrichtsarbeit können die Aufgaben 1–4 („Getting the message") in Kleingruppen erarbeitet werden. Es ist im Sinne der Binnendifferenzierung von der Lehrkraft zu erwägen, ob die vier Aufgaben in einer Gruppe auf unterschiedliche Gruppenmitglieder abgestellt werden. Insgesamt sollte jedoch jede Gruppe die Ergebnisse vortragen können. Während die 1. Aufgabe gut lesbar auf einem Plakat oder einer Folie verschriftlicht werden kann, sind für die Aufgaben 2–4 Visualisierungen denkbar (beschriftete Zeichnungen, bildliche Darstellungen).
In jedem Fall sollten die besten Ergebnisse nach der Präsentationsphase in Form einer Bündelung abschließend diskutiert und gewürdigt werden.
Die Aufgaben 5–7 führen zu ergiebigen Sprechanlässen und sollten deshalb in einem offenen Unterrichtsgespräch angegangen werden. Abhängig vom Leistungsstand empfiehlt sich eine Verschriftlichung von Beispielsätzen bei der Besprechung von Aufgabe 7. Der Aufgabenstellung folgend ist Aufgabe 8 in schriftlicher Form – in Stillarbeit oder als Hausaufgabe – zu erledigen.

Solutions

Activities p. 10

1. **Explain what this article is about in a couple of sentences.**
   (See the synopsis above.)

2. **What, in this context, is the "ultimate accessory"?**
   Name some other, less ultimate "accessories".
   The ultimate accessory is a baby.
   Other, less ultimate accessories would be handbags, shoes, sunglasses ('shades'), clothing brands, fast cars ...

3. **What would a "debut outfit" be? (l. 9)**
   The clothes the baby wears for his/her first "official" photos

4. **Can you think of two meanings for "clothes line"?**
   First meaning: the thing you hang the washing on
   Second meaning: a clothing brand

5. **How does the author feel about these celebrity mums?**
   Points that could be made:
   – She enjoys making fun of them.
   – On the other hand, they provide her with her subject.
   – She thinks they may deserve a bit of sympathy because any example of 'misbehaviour' will be criticized mercilessly.
   – But they exploit their babies for all they are worth.

6. **And how do you react to the text?**
   Personal views, which could include:
   – Celebrity mums 'earn' too much money.
   – They look very good.
   – They shouldn't exploit their babies like this.
   – It's fun to read about them.
   – It must be terrible/great to be a celebrity.
   – What have they done to deserve their fame?

7. **Comment on the photos.**
   Points that could be made:
   – Most photos obviously posed
   – Celebrities have to have a good figure.
   – Except when pregnant
   – Sunglasses more or less *de rigeur*
   – Maternal love has to be demonstrated if the baby is in the picture.

8. **This article came from a 'serious' Sunday newspaper. As you know, there are large number of magazines which deal with the life of 'celebs' – and plenty of people who want to buy them. Are you among them? To what extent do women (and men) like these deserve their fame and fortune? Write a paragraph about your own views, and discuss it with your fellow-students.**
   Personal views. A number of points which could be made appear above. Students should be encouraged to try and analyse the widespread fascination with the celebrity cult, and what could be described as our love-hate attitude to celebrities. They could wonder how someone can become 'famous for being famous' without any talent except spectacular looks.

When Information Rules

Karen Ross & Virginia Nightingale

Text

This text looks at the ways in which the once 'passive' audience consumed one medium at a time, to the modern age, where people are often plugged in to several different media at once, and can also take part in a two-way exchange of information, or become, for example, TV personalities themselves in programmes such as Big Brother.

Synopsis

The whole media environment has become much more complicated. Many homes have more than one television, many people listen to music on MP3 players, have mobile phones, play video games, etc. All this means that the concept of an 'audience' needs to be reinterpreted for the modern age. The new technologies enable people to access information in new ways, and become active participants or performers in the exchange of information and entertainment rather than passive consumers.

Unterrichtsempfehlungen

Der Text mit Aufgabenapparat ist gut zu Übungszwecken zu verwenden und überwiegend in Einzelarbeit zu erledigen bzw. vorzubereiten. Die Anregung zu Spekulationen unter „Before you read“ sollten zu Beginn der Arbeit mit dem Text als Hinführung eingesetzt werden und können nach der Lektüre mit den Textaussagen „abgeglichen“ werden. Folgende Punkte könnten von den Schülern genannt werden:

– Modern media
– Present-past comparisons
– Criticism/dangers of too much exposure to some media
– The role of the audience
– Phenomena such as Google, YouTube, Wikipedia etc.

Die „summaries“ könnten zudem in Kleingruppen vorgelesen werden, wobei jede Gruppe eine besonders gelungene „summary“ auswählt und später dem Plenum mit einer kurzen Begründung für die getroffene Wahl vorliest.
Die folgenden Aufgaben sollten in Einzelarbeit vorbereitet und dann im Rahmen von Unterrichtsgesprächen vertieft werden. Zur Beantwortung und Ergebnissicherung von Nr. 2 ist die Entwicklung eines Tafelbildes denkbar.

Solutions

Activities p. 11

1. **Make brief notes on the points mentioned by the authors, and turn them into a summary of about 100 words.**
   Points made:
   – Audience more complicated than in the past
   – Individual listening and viewing
   – Much larger media mix
   – Change in the concept of an audience
   – New media improve access to information
   – Emergence of reality TV (audience part of the media themselves)
   Summary: See the synopsis above

2. **What kind of book do you think *Media and Audiences* is? Use examples from the text to back up your view.**

Students should be able to surmise that this is an academic textbook for use by students on media studies courses.
Clues in the text:
- Balanced sentences, e.g. "Where once ... now ..."
- Careful formulations, e.g. "It is not unusual ..."
- Academic vocabulary, e.g. "the domestic norm", "proliferation"

3. **Have you read anything about further advances in information technology which are in the pipeline? How about ideas from science fiction?**
Some ideas:
- Chips implanted in our brains
- Virtual reality worlds
- Total surveillance of the population
- Sending objects – or people – from place to place via the Internet
- Merging of TV/computer/video etc.

Worksheet 1

Big Brother Is Watching *You*!

George Orwell

It was a bright cold day in April, and the clocks were striking thirteen. Winston Smith, his chin nuzzled into his breast in an effort to escape the vile wind, slipped quickly through the glass doors of Victory Mansions, though not quickly enough to prevent a swirl of gritty dust from entering along with him.

The hallway smelt of boiled cabbage and old rag mats. At one end of it a coloured poster, too large for indoor display, had been tacked to the wall. It depicted simply an enormous face, more than a metre wide: the face of a man of about forty-five, with a heavy black moustache and ruggedly handsome features. Winston made for the stairs. It was no use trying the lift. Even at the best of times it was seldom working, and at present the electric current was cut off during daylight hours. It was part of the economy drive in preparation for Hate Week. The flat was seven flights up, and Winston, who was thirty-nine and had a varicose ulcer[1] about his right ankle, went slowly, resting several times on the way. On each landing, opposite the lift-shaft, the poster with the enormous face gazed from the wall. It was one of those pictures which are so contrived that the eyes follow you about when you move. BIG BROTHER IS WATCHING YOU, the caption beneath it ran.

Inside the flat a fruity voice was reading out a list of figures which had something to do with the production of pig-iron[2]. The voice came from an oblong[3] metal plaque like a dulled mirror which formed part of the surface of the right-hand wall. Winston turned a switch and the voice sank somewhat, though the words were still distinguishable. The instrument (the telescreen, it was called) could be dimmed, but there was no way of shutting it off completely. [...] The telescreen received and transmitted simultaneously. Any sound that Winston made, above the level of a very low whisper, would be picked up by it; moreover, so long as he remained within the field of vision which the metal plaque commanded, he could be seen as well as heard.

From: George Orwell, *Nineteen eighty-four*, Penguin Books, Harmondsworth 1964 (1949)

---

[1] **varicose ulcer** a painful condition of the leg [2] **pig-iron** iron poured into moulds shaped like pigs
[3] **oblong** *rechteckig*

Activities

1. **Pick out some details which tell you about the standard of living in Winston's home town. When and/or where is/was life like that for ordinary people?**
2. **What could be the purpose of a 'Hate Week'?**
3. **How do we know that television was not widespread at the time when the book was written (1949)? What 'refinement' did the telescreen have which our televisions don't?**
4. **Would you expect the information about pig-iron production to be reliable? If not, why not?**

Worksheet 1

5. How are the mass media used by the Party, the group which runs the country, to control the citizens?

6. Are we in danger from too much surveillance in modern democracies?

7. Winston works in The Ministry of Truth. Can you imagine why this title is intended to be ironic?

8. Write a dialogue between a citizen of the country described in the text who is unhappy about the shortages, lack of freedom, constant surveillance etc., and a smooth administrator, who tries to convince him that this is actually for his own good (the expression 'jam tomorrow' is sometimes used to characterise systems where there is not much 'jam' today).

Worksheet 1 Solution

1. **Pick out some details which tell you about the standard of living in Winston's home town.**
   e. g. smells in the hallway, lifts not working, food poor quality, health bad, constant surveillance, even within the home
   When and/or where is/was life like that for ordinary people?
   The obvious case is in the former communist countries. Orwell is believed to have based some of his observations on life in wartime and post-war Britain.

2. **What could be the purpose of a 'Hate Week'?**
   Students could guess that the purpose would be to whip up hatred against 'the enemy'. People can be persuaded to accept a miserable life if it serves some higher purpose – such as defeating a real or imagined enemy.

3. **How do we know that television was not widespread at the time when the book was written (1949)? What 'refinement' did the telescreen have which our televisions don't?**
   If television had been familiar at the time, we can assume that Orwell would have used a two-way television rather than his 'telescreen'. The refinement is of course the ability to receive as well as transmit (cf. modern webcams).

4. **Would you expect the information about pig-iron production to be reliable?**
   If not, why not? It was a well-known feature of communist countries that favourable statistics of all kinds were published/broadcast, which often had no connection with reality.

5. **How are the mass media used by the Party, the group which runs the country, to control the citizens?**
   People are reminded that Big Brother is watching them wherever they go, and inside their flats they know that they are also being watched.

6. **Are we in danger from too much surveillance in modern democracies?**
   YES: surveillance cameras in public places, too much information about us available in electronic form, danger of identity theft, phone-tapping
   NO: surveillance helps to catch criminals, most people don't suffer from too much surveillance, only suspicious people likely to be targeted, we can only hope to catch terrorists by increasing surveillance

7. **Winston works in The Ministry of Truth. Can you imagine why this title is intended to be ironic.**
   We can safely assume that the job of the Ministry of Truth is to distort/spin/edit/repress information in the interests of the Party. It is actually the ministry of propaganda. Freedom of information would be out of the question.

8. **Dialogue**
   The dialogue could begin along these lines:
   Jane: Hi, Brian, no fresh fruit in the shops again today.
   Brian: Well, you know that our government has to save money.
   Jane: But the party bosses all have these huge black cars.
   Brian: It's the same in other countries.
   Jane: But ordinary people have cars too, in other countries ...

Newspapers and Teenage Magazines – the Shocking Truth

Vorbemerkungen zum Kapitel

Das Kapitel wird vielen Forderungen der aktuellen Fachdidaktik und der Curricula für die Sekundarstufe II gerecht. So kann anhand des Kapitels der intensive, kritische Umgang mit Textformaten der Druckmedien – der Presse der Zielkultur – sinnvoll geübt werden. Ferner wird durch das authentische Material (vgl. beispielsweise das Fotomaterial auf den Seiten 12–13 und S. 22) im Sinne der „cultural studies" die Sensibilität der Schülerinnen und Schüler für Gemeinsamkeiten und Unterschiede zwischen der eigenen Kultur und der Zielkultur gestärkt werden. Dabei wirkt sich besonders motivierend aus, dass das Kapitel vielfach sehr eng an die lebensweltlichen Interessen der Lernenden anknüpft. Artikelüberschriften wie z. B. „Not What Daddy Had in Mind" oder die Auseinandersetzung mit „Magazines for Teenagers" illustrieren diesen Zusammenhang.
Mithilfe von *Worksheet 2* sollen die Schüler angeleitet werden, einen eigenen Zeitungsartikel zu verfassen. Die Nachricht über Lewis Hamiltons Sieg in Monaco aus dem Sportteil der *Daily Mail* dient als Beispiel, um zu zeigen, wie dieser Artikel aussehen könnte. Dabei sollte das Augenmerk der Schüler auf folgende Punkte gelenkt werden;

- emotionale Sprache („sensational", „most coveted race in the world", „to wrest back the lead")
- alle wh-Fragen werden beantwortet (who, when, where, how, why)
- Gebrauch von direkter Rede
- die Besonderheit des Ereignisses wird hervorgehoben
- passender Schluss

Front Pages

Illustrations

This selection is intended to cover as wide a range as possible within the inevitable restraints. Fairly old and fairly new newspapers are represented, popular and serious, major and minor (even non-) events.

Unterrichtsempfehlungen

Die Schülerinnen und Schüler sollten zunächst Gelegenheit erhalten, das gezeigte Material zu betrachten und zu beschreiben. Eine Vorgehensweise, die zum einen schwächere Lernende aktiviert, sich in der Zielsprache zu beteiligen, zum anderen für den Kurs eine gemeinsame Basis zur weiteren Verständigung schafft. Es ist Aufgabe des Lehrers, zunächst darauf zu achten, dass eine systematische und genaue Beschreibung vorgenommen wird.
Danach kann dem Impuls unter „Comparing Front Pages" nachgegangen werden. Diese Phase sollte kurz ausfallen, da sie der Hinführung zum Thema und zu den Activities dient. Das Ergebnis der Umfrage war die Mondlandung 1969 (Evening Standard). Einer interessierten Schülerin/einem interessierten Schüler kann ein Kurzreferat über die British Library (http://www.bl.uk/) angeboten werden.
Die ersten beiden Aufgaben (What was it all about?) mit ihrer Rätselstimmung erfordern „detektivische" Arbeit und können gut in Partnerarbeit mit anschließender Ergebnissicherung im Plenum gelöst werden. Zusammen mit der *pre-reading activity* dürfte hiermit die Zeit einer 45-Minuteneinheit ausgefüllt sein.
Für die gründliche Bearbeitung der dritten Aufgabe (Serious – and not so serious) sollte eine weitere Unterrichtsstunde veranschlagt werden.

Es ist eine Überlegung wert, ob durch den Lehrer aktuelle „Front Pages“ den Schülerinnen und Schülern (z. B. per Beamer) zugänglich gemacht werden, damit eine Zuordnung leichter vorgenommen werden kann. Ferner könnte die Lehrkraft auf einem Arbeitsblatt einige Kriterien zur Identifizierung unterschiedlicher Zeitungstypen bereitstellen (diese Vorgehensweise wird durch die Leistungsstärke eines Kurses vorgegeben). Zentrale Ergebnisse sollten an der Tafel/auf einer Folie etc. gesichert werden.
„A bit of research“ (Aufgaben 4 und 5) sollten auch im Hinblick auf den an den Universitäten geforderten Kompetenzen von Schülerinnen und Schülern zu Hause oder aber an für Lernende zugänglich gemachten PCs der Schule bearbeitet werden. Die Lehrkraft sollte mit den Lernenden in jedem Fall Strategien zur effizienten Internetrecherche besprechen.
Vor dem Hintergrund eines neuen Erlasses zum bilingualen Unterricht in NRW ist es nunmehr möglich, einzelne Unterrichtsreihen/Module in verschiedenen Fächern anzubieten (Ähnliches ist auch in anderen Bundesländern durchführbar). Eine bilinguale Unterrichtsreihe im Fach Kunst, in der die Arbeit „Your front page“ bearbeitet werden kann, liegt nun im Bereich des Möglichen. Hier ist eine frühzeitige Absprache zwischen den Fachschaften erforderlich.
Eine Veröffentlichung – z. B. auf der Hompepage der Schule – sollte berücksichtigt werden. Es wird damit ein Anwendungsbezug bzw. eine Produktpräsentation hergestellt.

Solutions

Activities p. 13

1. **You won't be able to read the small print, but you should be able to write a sentence or two saying what each of these front pages was about**
   1. the moon landing in 1969, 2. the sinking of the General Belgrano during the Falklands War, 3. the British retreat from France via the Dunkirk beaches near the start of World War 2. 4. a political scandal, 5. an unlikely story in a tabloid newspaper, 6. a miscarriage of justice, 7. the 9-11-attacks, 8. the end of IRA-terrorism

2. **What, apart from the dates, tells you that two of the newspapers were much older than the others?**
   – Black and white photos
   – Yellowing paper
   – Smaller headlines than nowadays in popular papers

3. **It's not always easy to decide (on the basis of a single front page) which of these newspapers is or was serious, popular – or somewhere in between. What do you think?**
   Evening Standard – semi-popular (size of headlines, not terribly sensational)
   Sun – definitely popular, use of slang, very large headline, totally one-sided attitude to the sinking
   Daily Sketch (as for *Evening Standard*)
   The Guardian (obviously serious, small headline, a lot of small print on the front page)
   Sun (as above, plus treatment of a totally unimportant but sensational 'story' as the main 'news' item)
   Daily Mail (semi-popular, large headline, but a serious topic – note the top headline referring to St. Valentine's day – Feb. 14, the date of the paper)
   The Daily Telegraph (best-selling serious newspaper, relatively large headlines and photograph as a reaction to the enormity of the event, but note the detailed reporting in small print at the bottom of the page)
   The Independent (serious newspaper, making dramatic use of space to emphasise a point, fairly small photograph – a popular newspaper would have blown it up to fill the space – but large headlines)

4. **You should be able to find out whether these newspapers are left, right or centre on the political scale.**
   Evening Standard: right of centre
   Sun right wing but has lower class readership
   Daily Sketch: right of centre, could not compete with the *Mirror*, closed/merged with the *Daily Mail* in 1971
   The Guardian: left of centre with liberal sympathies
   Daily Mail: right of centre
   The Daily Telegraph: well to the right but still responsible – not at all 'far right' in its views
   The Independent: As the title implies, this newspaper tries very hard to avoid political bias either to the left or the right.

5. **Use the Internet to find out which major British daily newspapers do not feature on the previous page.**
   Daily Express, The Times (both politically on the right), *Daily Mirror* (left wing)
   Daily Star: not a proper newspaper; deals with celebrities, sport and TV plus 'page 3 girls'

6. **Choose a major event, past or present, fact or fiction, and compose your own front page for one of the English newspapers, serious or popular.**
   Free answer

Press Freedom

Nick Cohen

Author and text

Nick Cohen is a respected, often controversial journalist with generally left of centre views. Here he is pointing out that respected British newspapers are sometimes rather too close to the views of the military dictatorship in Pakistan when it comes to the freedom of the press.

Synopsis

World Press Freedom Day in 2006 was not a success. It began well with a German editor defending freedom of expression. His newspaper had bravely printed the Danish cartoons of Muhammed (which caused a worldwide uproar among Muslims). Dr. Maleeha Lodhi, The Pakistani High Commissioner disagreed. In her view, journalists who did not show respect for her government and religion should rightly be sent to prison. The media in her country are definitely not free.
However, the contrast between Dr Lodhi's views and those of liberal journalists in the west is not so stark as it would at first appear. She quoted articles from serious English newspapers with approval. As far as religion is concerned, the Council of Europe is considering whether freedom of expression should include the right to offend religions.

Unterrichtsempfehlungen

Die Aufgabe 1 sollte schriftlich als Hausaufgabe zur Unterrichtsstunde erledigt werden. Zum einen wird hierdurch ein vertieftes Textverständnis erzielt, was für die Bearbeitung der folgenden Aufgaben notwendig ist. Zum anderen bietet sich die Art der Aufgabenstellung als funktionale schriftliche Übung an, auch um im Hinblick auf Klausuranforderungen „Schreibroutine" aufzubauen. Abhängig von der Leistungsstärke des Kurses ist eine kontrastive Sicherung der Kernpunkte an der Tafel denkbar. In leistungsstarken Kursen ist sicherlich auch eine Abstraktion der wichtigsten Kernthesen im Rah-

men eines Unterrichtsgespräches denkbar, bei dem die Schülerinnen und Schüler ihre Hausaufgaben gegebenenfalls vervollständigen.
Die methodische Vorgehensweise zur Bearbeitung von „Where do you stand?“ ergibt sich aus der Arbeitsanweisung. Die Notizen aus der Partnerarbeitsphase könnten auf einer Flipchart in Form einer Mindmap gesichert werden, um später noch einmal auf die Positionen der Lernenden zurückgreifen zu können. Beispielsweise könnte abgeglichen werden, ob die Schülerinnen und Schüler Bedarf für Modifikationen etc. sehen.
Die abschließende Aufgabe zum Text bedarf einer Vorarbeit. Die Schülerinnen und Schüler sollten sich mithilfe des Lehrers/der Lehrerin vorab informieren. Es ist nicht immer damit zu rechnen, dass die Lernenden wirklich wissen, welche religiöse Bedeutung das Tragen eines Schleiers für Menschen muslimischen Glaubens hat. Erst durch dieses Basiswissen ist mit einer sachlichen Auseinandersetzung zu rechnen. Vielleicht ist hier auch ein Kurzreferat durch eine Mitschülerin/einen Mitschüler muslimischen Glaubens möglich, oder aber eine Zusammenarbeit mit der Fachschaft Religion denkbar. Weitere Cartoons zum Thema finden sich im Internet z. B. unter www.cagle.com.

Solutions

Activities p. 15

1. **Outline the views expressed by the editor of *Die Welt* and the Pakistani High Commissioner, making clear the contrast between the two views.**

High Commissioner	Editor
Does not accept that journalists have the right to offend foreign governments Demands ‘respect’, approves of punishment for ‘offending’	Defended freedom of expression, even if religious groups were offended Did not regret printing the controversial cartoons

2. **Make notes on your own views on press freedom and discuss the problem with your fellow students. Is it permissible to print almost anything, however offensive, because we believe in freedom of speech, or do we have to draw the line somewhere? If so, where? How about blasphemy, printing something which will bring down death threats on the writer’s head – or the right to privacy?**
   Points that could be made:
   - We already have libel laws – but only rich people can afford to go to court.
   - Most people accept that everyone has the right to some privacy – but how about celebrities who court publicity and then complain about intrusion, or dishonest politicians/business people?
   - If Muslims in particular care so much about respect for their religion, perhaps we should be at least very tactful when dealing with it – or should we be able to make fun of their religion, because we often make fun of western religions without the fear of sanctions (as a rule)?

3. **There are debates in most western countries about Muslim women wearing the veil in public or at work. Use the cartoon on p. 16 as a starting point for a discussion of the issues involved.**
   Points that could be made:
   - Clearly not possible to identify a woman wearing a niqab or burqa
   - The normal head scarf is seen by most Muslims as a standard part of their dress
   - To many non-Muslims it looks like a sign of repression/inequality between the sexes
   - Some forms of Muslim female dress make it difficult to lead what we would call a normal life
   - Westerners find it off-putting that only the eyes can be seen through a niqab. We use facial expression to interpret a person’s mood, reactions etc.

Scoop

Evelyn Waugh

Author

Students will find plenty of information about Waugh on the Internet. It is worth mentioning here that he has written a number of real masterpieces in his own inimitable style, e.g. *Decline and Fall, The Loved One, Brideshead Revisited*. The first name *Evelyn* is more usually a girls' name.

Synopsis (first extract)

Lord Copper claims that he does not try to influence his journalists, but then makes it quite clear that they have to not only support the side in any conflict which he supports, but that that side must win after some dramatic reporting on the progress of the war. He expects Boot to start submitting material very soon after he arrives. He should soon be able to report the first victory.

Unterrichtsempfehlungen

Die ersten drei Aufgaben können in einer Unterrichtsstunde bearbeitet werden, sofern eine Vorablektüre – z. B. als vorbereitende Hausaufgabe – geleistet worden ist. Aufgabe 1 kann in einem erarbeitenden Unterrichtsgespräch angegangen werden, bei dem in Stichpunkten die relevanten „requirements“ an der Tafel gesammelt werden.
In arbeitsteiligen Kleingruppen (in größeren Kursen erhalten jeweils 2 Kleingruppen den gleichen Aspekt) sollte Aufgabe 2 vorbereitet werden, um anschließend Ergebnisse in einem 3 Kategorien umfassenden Tafelbild zu sichern.
Die im Rahmen der ersten und zweiten Aufgabe geleistete Arbeit führt dann zum Abschluss der Stunde zu einer differenzierten Diskussion, da die Lernenden bei ihren Stellungnahmen auf erarbeitete Inhalte zurückgreifen können – je nach Kurskultur sollte die Lehrerin/der Lehrer immer wieder auf begründete Positionen insistieren.
Aufgabenstellung 4 dient zur Bearbeitung im Rahmen einer schriftlichen Hausarbeit.

Solutions

Activities p. 16

1. **How is Boot expected to report on the war? Make a list of the requirements laid down by his boss.**
   - plenty of 'news'
   - support the Patriots 100 %
   - a quick victory
   - plenty of exciting stories
   - a good full-length dispatch shortly after arrival
   - a victory about the middle of July

2. **How does Lord Copper regard the following?**
   – The British public
   wants exciting news all the time, otherwise soon gets bored
   – The 'right' kind of war
   the side he supports must win, it shouldn't drag on too long, there should be plenty of exciting stories and victories, culminating in a colourful takeover of the capital city
   – The facts
   are irrelevant unless they coincide with his views

3. **What is Evelyn Waugh's opinion of the popular press?**
He takes a very dim view of it. He thinks it is subject to the whims of the newspaper barons who own the newspapers, and will do almost anything to keep its readers entertained, with absolutely no respect for truth and honesty.

4. **Of course his views are exaggerated for comic effect, but perhaps there is a grain of truth in them. What do you think? Write a paragraph about the popular press in Germany.**
Points which could be made:
– The *Bildzeitung* will inevitably be the main target.
– Huge circulation – no serious competitors (British situation different – *Sun* and *Mirror* competing and on different sides politically)
– Bad reputation for hounding people, 'attributing' statements to people who did not make them, misquoting etc.
– Loves scandals, intruding into private lives, photos of scantily-dressed girls
– Has little respect for the truth
– Important people often choose to make statements via *Bild* in spite of its reputation
– On the right of the political spectrum in line with the views of the Springer empire.
– 'Serious' news takes up a lot less space than scandals, sensations and sports.

Synopsis (second extract)

A reporter called Jakes got out of the train at the wrong station on his way to report on a revolution, and immediately wrote a dramatic story about the fighting. His colleagues were surprised to get this report from the wrong country, but they printed the story anyway, and there were soon other reporters on the scene, also writing fictional reports. This caused so much panic in the country concerned that a real revolution was soon under way.

Unterrichtsempfehlungen

„The power of the press“ kann im Rahmen einer anwendungsbezogenen Unterrichtssequenz, z. B. innerhalb einer kleinen Projektphase, die 3–4 Wochenstunden umfasst, erarbeitet werden. Die ersten beiden Aufgaben bereiten diese Phase vor; des Weiteren sollte eine klare Zielperspektive und eine Vorgehensweise mit den Schülerinnen und Schülern festgelegt werden. Es empfiehlt sich, die Ergebnisse zu „The power of the press“ nicht nur im Kurs präsentieren zu lassen, sondern vielmehr dies vor einem Parallelkurs durchzuführen. Eine Auswertung der Ergebnisse und eine Abstraktion der wichtigsten Erkenntnisse in schriftlicher Form sollte den Prozess folgerichtig abschließen und kann wieder im Plenum des Kurses vorgenommen werden.

Solutions

Activities p. 17

1. **Re-tell the story about Jakes in five or six sentences.**
See the synopsis above

2. **Why do you think the seasoned reporter says '*You know*' after characterising the style of Jakes' report from the 'war zone'?**
The items mentioned by the reporter amount to a list of common clichés used by reporters writing about war. (Just because they are clichés, it doesn't mean, unfortunately, that they have no basis in fact.)

3. **To what extent do you think that newspapers can influence events as well as reporting on them? Can you think of any examples?**
   Points that could be made:
   – By choosing which events to report on, newspapers (and TV/radio) decide what is news and what isn't.
   – At any time wars are going on in faraway places which we hear and read nothing about, so there is no sense of outrage, very little aid etc. Wars which are reported on receive far more attention of every kind from governments and the public.
   – It is generally agreed that reporting on the Vietnam War (particularly on TV in this case), helped to bring the war to an end when Americans saw what conditions were like for their soldiers.

4. **The popular press does not have a very good reputation among educated people, but it sells a lot more copies than the so-called broadsheets or serious newspapers. What makes the popular newspapers so popular?**
   Some points which could be made:
   – easy to read (short articles, large print)
   – dramatic/sensational reporting
   – everything turned into an interesting 'story'
   – appeals to popular tastes by reporting on celebrities, scandals, sport etc.
   – avoid 'difficult' topics in the field of politics etc. unless they can be turned into an easily-digested story

5. **Buy one or two copies of popular newspapers in Germany (or English popular newspapers if available locally). Describe some good and bad features, scanning or cutting out material and putting it in your report to illustrate the points you make.**
   Individual creative activity

Not What Daddy Had in Mind!

Amanda Cable

Text

This is a classic example of a human interest story from a semi-popular newspaper. It also raises a number of questions about the characters involved and their long-term chances of happiness together.

Synopsis

The text begins with a description of a typical day in the life of Sue Chinolo, an Englishwoman living in Tanzania with her African husband and baby daughter.
Her life is basic, even primitive, and very different from her early years in a prosperous English family, and later as a hotel manager. Her husband Shadrack grew up in a mud hut, and was often hungry as a child.
Sue was not satisfied with her life as a hotel manager, so she decided to take a job as a tour guide in Africa. It was in Zanzibar that she met her future husband, who had worked his way up to managing a hotel.
She was very taken with his big smile, and after spending the better part of a night talking by a campfire on the beach, they fell in love. Sue had to leave Zanzibar, but kept in touch with Shadrack by e-mail.
Shadrack proposed marriage before Sue left after her next visit, and was immediately accepted. She returned home to tell her father, who took the news very well. Then she returned to Zanzibar to get married and begin her new life.
Shadrack thinks she has fitted in very well in Africa, but she has found it tough and lonely. Other African husbands do not want their wives to be friends with Sue and become westernised. She was annoyed by the way her husband just came and went, but

he has agreed to tell her when he is leaving. She does not go out at night, and has to be very careful about travelling alone.
Basic services are not reliable and they are often short of food, but the arrival of their daughter Melody has made it all seem worthwhile. Sue thinks her daughter is enjoying a natural, unspoilt childhood, and her husband makes her feel like the richest woman in the world.

Unterrichtsempfehlungen

Eine Vorablektüre des Textes ist unumgänglich, um den Unterrichtsprozess zeitlich zu entlasten. Die Schülerinnen und Schüler sollten den Text zu Hause lesen und dabei stichwortartig die Fragen und Impulse am Rand beantworten bzw. nachgehen. Die Bearbeitung der ersten beiden Aufgaben sollte dann in Partnerarbeit im Unterricht vorgenommen werden, da hiermit ein vertieftes Textverständnis erzielt wird, welches für die Weiterarbeit erforderlich ist.
Die Ergebnispräsentation zur dritten Aufgabe ist in Form einer kleinen Szene denkbar. Auf der Grundlage der aus dem Text erschlossenen Gegensätze stellen sich Sue bzw. Shadrack ihren Schwiegereltern vor. Eine Befragung durch die Schwiegereltern ist möglich. Das Publikum erhält den Auftrag die eigenen Aufzeichnungen zu ergänzen und die „Aufführung“ zu kommentieren.
Sollte die Lehrerin/der Lehrer sich für eine Ergebnispräsentation in Form einer szenischen Darstellung entscheiden, so ist für den durch die ersten drei Aufgaben vorskizzierten Prozess ein Zeitumfang von einer Doppelstunde einzuplanen.
Die Aufgaben 4 und 5 sind in einer Unterrichtsstunde zu lösen. Sie fördern insbesondere einen kritischen Umgang mit Texten der Printmedien. Sie können gut in Form von Unterrichtsgesprächen mit anschließender Ergebnissicherung (an der Tafel oder in Form einer mündlichen Zusammenfassung durch die Lehrkraft) gelöst werden. Die letzten beiden Aufgaben des Apparates vertiefen die geleistete Arbeit und sollten im Rahmen einer schriftlichen Hausaufgabe von den Schülerinnen und Schülern bearbeitet werden.

Solutions

While-reading task p. 17

What are your first impressions of the headline – and the photo?
Some possible reactions:
- Photo shows a racially mixed couple – they seem very happy, is the baby happy, too?
- possible cultural problems
- Some fathers/families might have problems with a black son-in-law.
- She's much taller than him – does it matter?
- Which country do they live in?
- How did they meet?

While-reading task p. 18

What facts tell us that Sue is an upper-middle class woman?
- smart Surrey home
- privately educated
- speaks with a 'clipped' (posh, upper-class) accent
- high-flying career woman
- father's restrained reaction to the news of her engagement
- father drives a Mercedes

While-reading tasks p. 19

Why do you think Sue ended up as a tour guide?

- She thought there must be more to life than hotel management/closing business deals/making profits.
- She thought she was never going to get married, so decided on adventure instead of domesticity.

What exactly attracted Sue to Shadrack – and vice versa?

She liked his big smile, energy, engaging laugh, and talking to him (no doubt finding a lot of common ground in spite of cultural differences), incredible appetite for life, unfailing optimism.

We know that Shadrack fell in love with her, and cannot have been thinking along materialistic lines as she has to share his life and not vice versa. Exactly what attracted him to her is not made clear.

While-reading tasks p. 20

How would you expect Sue's father to react to the news of Sue's engagement?

He was probably hoping his daughter would get married one day, but like most parents he would have wanted her to marry the classic 'nice young man' from the same kind of background as his own family.

To what extent do you think Sue will really have "fitted in perfectly"?

As long as she is happy with her husband and baby, and does not mind the hardship, she can be said to have fitted in to some extent, but her loneliness, and the hostility of other African husbands (which means that their wives avoid her) could be a real problem. There is also a language barrier – presumably Shadrack can speak some English, but it is very unlikely that she can communicate with her neighbours.

While-reading task p. 21

An unspoilt childhood for Melody – or a deprived childhood?

Some points that could be made:

- can spend a lot of time playing on the beach (+)
- the joy of nature (+)
- will not grow up with DVDs and video games (+/–)
- family and love the centre of her life (+)
- more or less cut off from the outside world (–)
- will probably get a very basic education (–)
- a primitive way of life may not be good for her in various ways (–)
- may not be accepted by the other local children (–)

Activities p. 21

1. **Re-tell the story using once sentence for each 'step'. leaving a space after each step when you come to writ them down.**
2. **Now add people's reactions at each step, again using one sentence in each case.**
   Sue Chinolo is living the life of an African housewife in Tanzania.
   She has never been happier.
   She and her husband are a strikingly different couple in many ways.
   Everyone turns round to look at them.
   Sue gave up her job as a hotel manager to become a tourist guide.
   This brought her to Zanzibar, where she met Shadrack.
   They were both very happy to see one another and fell in love.
   Everyone else went to bed.
   On Sue's next visit to Zanzibar, Shadrack proposed.
   Sue's father took the news calmly (he may have been hiding his real feelings).
   Shadrack told his parents he was marrying a Western girl.
   They were thrilled. They had been worried that he would never find a wife.
   Shadrack thinks his wife fits in perfectly.
   In fact she is lonely and find the life tough. Other African husbands disapprove of her and don't want their wives to make friends with her.

Sue has had a baby daughter, Melody.
Both parents think Melody has 'sealed their happiness'. Sue is very happy that her daughter will be having what she sees as an unspoilt childhood.

3. **Find as many contrasts as you can between Sue and Shadrack (appearance, previous life, education, parents ...) and set them out in two columns.**

Sue	Shadrack
– white	– black
– blonde	– black hair
– tall	– short
– private school	– basic education
– upper-class family	– very poor family
– father an traditional, prosperous Englishman	– father scraped a living
– nice house in Surrey	– two-room mud hut
– worked as a hotel manager	– also a hotel manager, but before that worked as a goatherd and made coathangers from scrap metal

4. **The *Daily Mail* is usually described as semi-popular newspaper, so the style of the article 'should' be semi-sensational. Is it? Find it and talk about typical stylistic features of the article.**
In fact the article is not particularly sensational, although the subject matter 'asks for' a fairly sensational approach. In a really popular newspaper there would probably be some racist undertones, but this is not the case.
Note careful formulations such as "... could be described as primitive".
Typical stylistic features:
– use of contrast
– a good deal of description (both people and background)
– a lot of vocabulary referring to happiness etc., e.g. has never been happier, huge grin, smile, lit up his whole face, engaging laugh, warm and safe, felt so blessed to be alive

5. **Almost inevitably, an article of this kind makes use of some very well-worn clichés. List them, and try to decide whether you would say that the article is racist.**
See the tabular information under question 3. Although these clichés and contrasts could be interpreted in a racist way, it would be hard to find evidence for racism in the article. It seems as if the author genuinely believes that Sue has found happiness with her African husband and little daughter – happiness which had eluded her in her earlier life.

6. **A reader commented, "The two main characters in the story emerge as really nice people." What evidence can you find for (or against) this view?**
Sue:
– appreciates nature
– does not mind living a primitive kind of life
– loves and cares for her daughter
– loves and is loyal to her husband
– not affected by major racial and cultural differences
– prepared to give up her career and try to find a life which suits her
– independent, speaks her mind (although this does not go down well in her new community)
– (negative – perhaps rather naïve, may not have looked very far into the future)
Shadrack:
– energetic
– happy smile

- 'incredible appetite for life'
- unfailing optimism
- loves and is loyal to his wife
- (negative – underestimates his wife's problems, comes and goes as he pleases)

7. **Most people would enjoy reading this story because of its 'fairy-tale' elements – but would this couple really 'live happily ever after'? Write a paragraph in which you try to answer this question from a personal point of view.**
   Points which could be made:
   - they definitely love and respect one another now – may or may not be 'until death us do part'
   - their daughter – and possibly other children – may help to hold the marriage together
   - the two characters seem to be complementary – not just a physical relationship
   - may still be in a kind of 'honeymoon period'. If and when it is over, Sue may come down to earth with a bump when she fully realises that her primitive way of life is permanent
   - Shadrack may come to resent her western-style independence
   - Sue may come to resent his (implicitly sexist) comings and goings whenever he feels like it
   - differences in culture/family background/education may start to cause problems which are under the surface at present

Magazines for Teenagers

Pictures and texts

Typical examples of a small number of magazines which are known to be popular with teenage boy and girls respectively were collected and subjected to an informal analysis and comparison. No claims are made with respect to statistical accuracy, but anyone purchasing one of the magazines referred to will find the contents match these results quite closely.

Unterrichtsempfehlungen

Der Einstieg in den abschließenden Teil des Kapitels zu „Newspapers and Teenage Magazines" erfolgt mithilfe des Bildmaterials auf der Seite 22. Die Zusammenstellung sollte für Spontanreaktionen, Spekulationen, aber auch zur Übung von Bildbeschreibung eingesetzt werden. Mögliche Themen der Magazine lassen sich an der Tafel auflisten, dabei können auch die Bilder auf den Seiten 23 und 24 verwendet werden:

likely topics

boys: football, cars, girls, trainers, computers, phones
girls: celebrities, boys, fashion, make-up, questionnaires

Da das Thema sehr motivierend an die Lebenswelt und den Erfahrungsschatz von Jugendlichen anknüpft, dürften sich vielfältige Sprechanlässe ergeben, bei denen die Lernenden auf ihren persönlichen Umgang und Erfahrungsschatz mit ähnlichen Magazinen zurückgreifen werden. Es ist daher möglich, schon in dieser Phase Anregungen aus der Aufgabe 8 auf Seite 24 ergänzend aufzugreifen – beispielsweise als vorbereitende Hausaufgabe. Als Alternative ist denkbar, dass der Lehrer eigenes, aktuelles Material, welches er bei Urlaubsreisen in Länder der Zielkulturen gesammelt hat, mit in den

Unterricht bringt und auf Kleingruppen verteilt. Beschreibung, Kategorisierung (boys' and girls'), Vergleich mit deutschsprachigen Jugendmagazinen und Stellungnahmen könnten dabei eine Zielperspektive für eine kurze Arbeitsphase in Kleingruppen bilden. Die Angaben Girls' Mags/Boys' Mags bieten auf der einen Seite eine interessante Möglichkeit zu kontroversen Diskussionen, auf der anderen Seite aber auch eine exemplarische Trainingsmöglichkeit im Hinblick auf den Umgang mit ähnlichen Auflistungen (der Umgang mit tabellarischen Auflistungen, Grafiken, Schaubildern ist als Vorbereitung auf das Zentralabitur in NRW erforderlich). Der Lehrende sollte daher besonders darauf achten, den Lernenden treffendes Vokabular und geeignete Phrasen zur Beschreibung und Diskussion des vorhandenen Materials zur Verfügung zu stellen. Die schriftlich auszuführenden Aufgaben des Aufgabenapparates sollten daher je nach Leistungsvermögen des Kurses im Unterrichtsgespräch vorentlastend angegangen werden, um insbesondere den Gebrauch notwendigen Sprachmaterials einzuüben. Neben den Schreibaufträgen, die in Form von Hausaufgaben erledigt werden können, bietet sich für die Aufgabe zwei eine Phase der Partnerarbeit an, wobei es sicherlich spannend wäre, die Partnerpaare möglichst aus einem Schüler und einer Schülerin zu bilden. Ähnliches ließe sich für die Aufgaben unter „Popular culture or 'popular' culture?" initiieren (ein ähnliches Arrangement in Kleingruppen ist dabei denkbar). Ferner könnten die Fragen 5, 6, 7 und 8 in Form eines Interviews mit einem Experten umgestaltet und präsentiert werden. Zentrale und tragfähige Aspekte aus dem Interview sollten abschließend an der Tafel unter der Überschrift „Popular culture or popular 'culture'?" gesichert werden.

Solutions

Activities p. 24

1. **Write short paragraphs explaining what the reader is likely to find in typical magazines for teenage boys and girls.**
   All the necessary material is available on pages 24–26.
   Some useful expressions:
   A typical English magazine for teenager boys/girls would contain ...
   There is a lot of material on ...
   I did (not) expect to find ...
   If we compare ...
   Other topics which are also dealt with are ...
   On the whole ...
   To sum up ...

2. **Make notes on items in the magazines for your own and the opposite sex which you find surprising, not at all surprising, annoying, shocking, etc.**
   Boys may mention the human interest stories for girls, the advice on dealing with boyfriends and the amount of space given to fashion, beauty and celebrities.
   Girls will probably mention the photos of semi-naked women in the boys' magazines, the tasteless 'news' stories, the almost total lack of any help for dealing with the opposite sex.

3. **Discuss your findings in class.**
   Some useful expressions:
   Trust boys/girls to want to look at/read about ...
   I'm (not) (really) surprised that ...
   I wouldn't dream of (reading about/looking at) ...
   Why on earth do boys/girls want to ...
   I would never buy a magazine which ...
   What kind of people would buy ...

4. **Make lists of similarities and differences between the two kinds of magazines. Turn your notes into a paragraph and add your own view on this kind of material.**
   Similarities
   free gifts, celebrities, photos of attractive young men/women quite a lot of advertisements, some puzzles, competitions, etc.
   Differences
   The photos of women in the boys' magazines are more or less 'soft porn', the advertisements are for different kinds of goods, no articles on cars for girls, no TV schedules for girls, far less interest among the girls for photos of the opposite sex, no horrific news stories, technical information or sports news for girls, very little help with personal/social problems for boys, no human interest stories for boys, ...

5. **All kinds of elements from the broader cultural spectrum are entirely missing from these magazines. What kind of elements? Is it simply snobbish to expect 'serious' music, literature etc. to be covered?**
   Sample answers:
   - Missing elements: classical music, modern literature, politics, advice on dealing with smoking/drugs/alcohol/money problems
   - It is snobbish, only a tiny minority is interested in that kind of stuff.
   - These magazines are good examples of 'dumbing down' – providing entertainment for the lowest common denominator.
   - Plenty of teenagers read 'good' books – it wouldn't do any harm to include some 'serious' book/film reviews.

6. **What do these magazines tell us about education in English schools?**
   It's dangerous to speculate, of course, but we would have to say that the schools have failed to interest anyone who buys and reads these magazines in anything of an 'educational' nature. There are plenty of other newspapers/magazines available, dealing with the full range of leisure and other interests, but they are not produced specifically for teenagers, although plenty of teenagers read them.

7. **The magazines for boys were far thicker than the magazines for girls. Why might this be?**
   Possible reasons (the first and second (?) are deliberately sexist/controversial):
   - girls have a shorter attention span (!)
   - girls may prefer a number of shorter items
   - the TV guide and sports information take up a lot of pages in the boys' magazines
   - so do the photos of girls
   - boys may be prepared to spend more on their magazines

8. **Is the situation any different in Germany? Bring some German teenage magazines into school and produce information about the content in tabular form, using the tables for the English magazines as a guide. Discuss your findings.**
   Individual or group work. It seems likely that German magazines are in some ways much more frank/less prudish in dealing with health/sex issues.

   A teacher came into an English classroom during an German exchange scheme, and found the English teenagers gathered round a copy of Bravo which one of the German students had brought in. When the teacher saw what they were reading about/looking at, she was shocked, and confiscated the magazine.

   This little anecdote could be used to get the discussion going. What kinds of material do teenagers need/want to read about? Are they getting it?

Worksheet 2

Writing a News Story

Good journalists provide you with the best models for your own written English – after all, you aren't in the business of trying to write a new 'Hamlet' or 'Oliver Twist' – best to leave that kind of thing to the natives.
Good journalists are not just good at the language, they're good at getting and keeping the reader's interest – if they don't succeed, they'll soon be looking for a new job. And this applies as much for the 'respectable' newspapers as it does for the tabloids. As somebody once said, "That book is good in vain which the reader throws away". Well, a news story is a rather specific kind of text, so here's some help in planning and writing a good one.

Activities

1. Make sure you find a good topic to start with. If possible, it should be a real topic, in the news at present or recently. The topic should not be too complicated, or it will be hard to deal with in this format.

2. Try to answer the so-called 'wh-questions' near the beginning: what, who, how, when, where, and a bit further into the article, why.

3. Use some of the standard devices which journalists employ to make their material interesting, and give it authority, e. g.
   – direct speech from people involved and also from experts (policemen, doctors, politicians)
   – Use emotive or sensational language where appropriate.
   – Begin 'in medias res' if appropriate (i. e. start with an interesting or exciting detail, then go back to tell the story chronologically).
   – Don't give everything away at the start: "Make 'em laugh, make 'em cry, make 'em *wait*."
   – Find ways to make this event seem special, out of the ordinary (otherwise it's not worth writing about). Dog bites man – no story. Man bites dog – it's a story!
   – Try to find a conclusion which really 'rounds your story off'.
   Here's a brief sports report to show you how it's done:

Worksheet 2

This will always be my best win, says Hamilton

Jonathan McEvoy

Lewis Hamilton achieved a 17-year dream by joining a roll-call[1] of Formula One greats with a sensational victory in yesterday's Monaco Grand Prix.
The 23-year-old became only the fifth Briton to win the most coveted[2] race in the world, surviving an early crash and tricky wet conditions to wrest back[3] the lead in the driver's championship.
Hamilton was ecstatic as he reflected on emulating Ayrton Senna, the late Brazilian world champion he worshipped as a six-year-old boy new to karting.
'This is the best win ever, for sure,' he said. 'Even if I were to win here again, which I plan on doing, this will always be the best one. The first Monaco. Even though I didn't get pole, I just stayed optimistic and brought it home. It was the most fun I've had in a race ever.
'From the last corner on, I was screaming my head off basically, making sure the radio was off, but just so happy I was able to pull it off.
'I said to you all that this is my favourite circuit. This is the one that I would want to win more than any other in the world!'

Jonathan McEvoy, "This will always be my best win, says Hamilton", in: DAILY MAIL, 26.05.2008

---

[1] **roll-call** list [2] **to covet** to desire strongly [3] **to wrest back** to pull sth away violently

Advertising – Buy One, Get One Free

Vorbemerkungen zum Kapitel

Das Kapitel „Advertising – Buy One, Get One Free“ ermöglicht eine differenzierte und kritische Auseinandersetzung mit der auf Schülerinnen und Schüler täglich einwirkenden Werbeindustrie und deren Strategien. Die oftmals daraus entstehenden Probleme werden ersichtlich. Die Auseinandersetzung mit dem Kapitel schafft eine sensibilisierte Wahrnehmung, da es multiperspektivisch auf „Werbung“ mit ihren Auswirkungen schaut. Die Lernenden können dabei in Distanz zu der sie immer und überall umgebenden Werbung gehen und im Idealfall lernen, den manipulativen Werbestrategien mit einem kritischen Bewusstsein entgegenzutreten.
Darüber hinaus leistet das Kapitel einen Beitrag zur Erweiterung der interkulturellen Handlungskompetenz, da es unterschiedliche Einblicke in das Alltagsleben der Zielkultur gewährt.

Where to Begin?

Text and illustrations

The idea here was to give a kind of lightning survey of advertising, pointing out the stock characters used by advertisers, their understanding of our psychological fears and weaknesses, and the things we want, even though we often won't admit it.
Students could collect and comment on as many examples as they can find for each of the categories referred to.

Onward Christian Admen

Text

Several British newspapers publish a third or fourth leader which is generally of a humorous nature. In this example, the ridiculous attempt of a local council to treat a Christian cross as an advertising symbol is used as a starting point for some speculation about other unusual 'advertisements'.

Synopsis

A council in the West Midlands has asked a local church to pay a fee for advertising because it has put up a cross outside the church. This could lead to flags and pedestrian crossings being treated as advertisements, too. The leader writer advises the minister of the church in question to make the symbol part of the actual building, as is the case with the Oxo tower and St Paul's Cathedral.

Unterrichtsempfehlungen

Über die Einführungsseite auf Seite 25 erfolgt eine generelle Orientierung in Bezug auf das Thema und eine Anknüpfung an die Lebenswelt der Lernenden. U.a. können die Zeichnungen auf Seite 25 sehr leicht von den Schülerinnen und Schülern mit aktuellen Werbebeispielen illustriert werden, da das Dargestellte sehr exemplarisch ist.
Die Definition links auf der Seite 26 sollte von den Lernenden in den Blick genommen werden, bevor es an die Lektüre des Artikels geht. Die ersten beiden Aufgaben des *leading articles* zielen auf die Sicherung des Textverständnisses ab und bereiten die analytisch ausgerichtete Aufgabe 3 vor, die gegebenenfalls auch im Rahmen einer schriftlichen Hausaufgabe erledigt werden kann. Alternativ könnten die Aufgaben 1 und 2 als Impuls herangezogen werden, die Schülerinnen und Schüler zur Erstellung von 2–3 kurzen True/False-Fragen in Gang zu setzen. Mithilfe einer Meldekette könnten sich

die Lernenden des Kurses dann ihre Fragen gegenseitig stellen, bis die zentralen Aspekte geklärt sind. Erstellung der Fragen und Durchführung der Meldekette bringen Abwechselung in den Unterricht und nehmen aufgrund des überschaubaren Umfangs des Textes nicht sehr viel Zeit in Anspruch.
Nr. 4 des Aufgabenapparates lädt zu einer Diskussion ein, wobei die Lernenden vor Beginn der Diskussion einige Minuten erhalten sollten, sich zu orientieren und sich möglicherweise mit dem Partner über Argumente auszutauschen. Die Diskussion sollte mit einer mündlichen Bündelung der tragfähigsten Argumente abgerundet werden. In leistungsstarken Kursen kann diese Bündelung von einer Schülerin/einem Schüler übernommen werden. Generell ist es jedoch empfehlenswert, dass sich die Lehrkraft während der Diskussion Notizen anfertigt, um vor dieser Folie eine Bündelung zentraler Aspekte in wertschätzender Weise vor dem Kurs vorzunehmen.
Die den Aufgabenapparat abschließende Aufgabe 5 setzt einen anwendungsorientierten Akzent. Die Schülerinnen und Schüler könnten beispielsweise mithilfe von Digitalkameras interessantes Material aus ihrer Stadt fotografieren/sammeln, auf Poster in Form einer Collage arrangieren und mit Kommentaren versehen. Das Ganze ließe sich im Foyer der Schule präsentieren.

Solutions

Activities p. 26

1. **There is a long tradition of short humorous leading articles in British newspapers. What is this one about?**
   It is about the ridiculous attempt of a local council to charge a church for putting up a cross outside.

2. **How does the writer suggest that the church in question could avoid paying the fee?**
   The church could make the cross part of the building so that it would not be seen as an advertisement by the council.

3. **What exactly makes the article humorous?**
   The author uses the following strategies to make the article humorous:
   – ridiculous comparisons, e.g. a cross in the sky is compared with the old slogan 'Go to work on an egg'
   – He suggests other, equally unlikely 'advertisements', e.g. taxing the Union flag.
   – He speculates that this could be the start of a trend – even a cross on top of a church may be taxed one day.

4. **Do you think the town council in Dudley was within its rights to try and impose a fee?**
   Most students will probably immediately say 'no', but we live in times when religions are hypersensitive about their rights. Perhaps the council was worried that other religions would want to set up large symbols as well, which could lead to complaints. It would also be interesting to try and draw a line between advertising symbols and 'other' symbols, such as the cross, flags, uniforms/badges of rank etc.

5. **Where does advertising begin and end? Look around you in town and try to find some interesting items to comment on.**
   Ideas:
   – texts on t-shirts
   – well-known symbols such as the Nike 'swoosh'
   – texts on carrier bags
   – banners across the street

– window displays
– special offers of all kinds
– traffic signs
– unusual and/or very large typefaces

"Misleading" Winston Milk Ads Pulled

Sarah-Kate Templeton

Text Lord Winston is a well-known scientist and television personality. He laid himself open to criticism by making claims for, and endorsing, a product which turned out not to do 'what it said on the label'. The journalist will no doubt have enjoyed 'taking him down a peg or two'. As a result of the Advertising Standards Authority's (ASA's) ruling, the advertisements have been 'pulled' (withdrawn).

Synopsis The ASA has ruled that advertisements for a brand of milk claimed to have high levels of omega-3 were misleading. The manufacturers have been forced to withdraw the advertisements, which had led to very good sales of the product.
These advertisements claimed that the milk may make children more intelligent because of its omega-3 additive.
Lord Winston made this claim in the advertisements on behalf of the manufacturers. The ASA's ruling will be seen as criticism of Lord Winston, and could damage his reputation. He still claims that omega-3 is very good for children, backing up his claim with references to scientific publications on the subject.
However, the ASA ruled that these benefits did not apply when the quantities of omega-3 in the milk were much smaller than in the scientific experiments. There was no evidence that such small quantities could be beneficial, unless children drank huge quantities of the milk. Winston and the manufacturers still believe the claims made to be true, but the manufacturers have agreed to amend their advertising accordingly.

Unterrichtsempfehlungen

Eine Hinführung zum Text wird über die Fotos auf Seite 27 und mit der Frage „How might advertisements for ‚clever milk' be misleading?" initiiert und kann in einem offenen Unterrichtsgespräch erfolgen. Folgendes Ergebnis ist denkbar:

"Parents, most of whom would like their children to do well, or even better in school, might easily think that clever milk would make their children cleverer."

Danach kann die Lektüre des Textes vorgenommen werden und eine Sicherung des Grobverständisses anhand der Fragen am Rand des Textes angegangen werden. Besonders in leistungsschwächeren Kursen empfiehlt sich ein gemeinsames sukzessives Vorgehen, während in leistungsstärkeren Kursen an eine Lektüre des Textes in Einzelarbeit zu denken ist. Die Beantwortung der Fragen am Rand kann dann in Zusammenarbeit mit einem Partner vorgenommen werden.
Diese Vorbereitung entlastet den Umgang mit dem Aufgabenapparat auf Seite 28, dessen Bearbeitung zum Teil eine sehr detailreiche Textkenntnis notwendig macht. Während die Aufgaben 1 und 4 in Form von Unterrichtsgesprächen mit abschließender mündlicher Bündelung zentraler Beantwortungsaspekte gelöst werden sollten, sind die Aufgaben 2 und 3 in Einzel- bzw. Partnerarbeit vorzubereiten und anschließend in einer frontal ausgerichteten Unterrichtsphase zu lösen, in der ein Tafelbild entstehen sollte, das tragfähige Ergebnisse zusammenführt.

Die Aufgaben 5 und 6 bieten sich schlüssig als Hausaufgabe an. In Bezug auf Aufgabe 5 sollten die Schüler ganz konkret Beispiele benennen und den Grund für ihre getroffene Wahl begründen können.

Solutions

While-reading tasks p. 27

Why do you think sales were 'buoyant' as a result of the campaign?
It is very likely that parents knew of and respected Lord Winston, so they bought the milk because they thought it would improve their children's intelligence.

What kind of person does Lord Winston seem to be?
He is a respected scientist, a peer, and also a very successful TV presenter. Judging from the photo, he seems to be a pleasant, humorous kind of person as well. However, it is likely that in this case he allowed the milk producer to exploit his reputation for its own purposes. He may himself have fallen in love with his own image to some extent. In advertising terms, we tend to believe what scientists tell us in advertisements, whether they wear white coats or, as in this case, an open-necked shirt. Winston is so well-known that he doesn't need a white coat (usually worn by actors pretending to be scientists/doctors in any case).

While-reading tasks p. 28

Why all this science?
Winston probably has a bad conscience over his role in this affair, so he quotes over 200 learned articles to back up the claims. We call this process "blinding us with science". If all these scientists say omega-3 is good for us, it must be true. But they all refer to 'high doses' of the additive, not the very small quantities in the milk.

Activities p. 28

1. **What did Lord Winston agree to do?**
He agreed to appear in advertisements for milk with added omega-3. He endorsed the manufacturer's claims that it would make children more intelligent. He even allowed them to hang a label saying 'clever milk' on the bottle he was holding.

2. **What was the result a) for sales of the product?**
b) in the wider context?
a) Sales of the milk were 'buoyant', i. e. very good.
b) The ASA became suspicious of the claims, decided they were not justified, and asked the manufacturer to withdraw the advertisements.

3. **Why exactly did the ASA object to the adverts?**
They pointed out that *large quantities* of omega-3 had improved the intelligence of *children with learning difficulties*. There was no evidence that there would be the same result for *normal children* taking in *very small quantities*.

4. **How would you assess Lord Winston's role?**
He probably enjoyed the publicity until the ASA stepped in. He may not be entirely honest in claiming that he still believes the amount of omega-3 in the milk could have a beneficial effect. He probably wishes he had not got involved.

5. **Have you come across advertising which strikes you as misleading in Germany?**
Students should be directed towards claims for patent medicines, cosmetics and alcohol as good starting points.

6. **What features of this campaign link up with the material about advertising on the first page of this unit?**
Some suggestions:
– Someone holding up a bottle or packet (in the original ad).
– Scientist used to give credibility to the claims.

– Winston also a well-known TV personality
– fear of not being good parents

Pencil Case With a Playboy Bunny Logo Is Banned by School

James Mills

Text This text can be seen as a kind of debate. Did the teachers do the right thing by banning a pencil case with the Playboy logo, or were they overreacting? Did the pencil case only become 'inappropriate' when a fuss was made about it?

Synopsis A young girl, Karla Anthony, took her new pencil case to school and proudly showed it to her friends. She particularly liked the 'bunny' logo, but when teachers saw it, they recognized it as the Playboy logo, and banned the pencil case from the school as inappropriate. The girl's parents said that the school should never have made an issue of it. For their daughter the logo was just a pink bunny, but now they would have to explain to her about Playboy magazine. They intend to ignore the school ban, which they regard as ridiculous. WH Smith, which sold the pencil case, claimed that the Playboy logo had lost some of its 'adult' connotations over the last few years, and become a popular fashion brand.

Unterrichtsempfehlungen

Der Text mit seinem Aufgabenapparat eignet sich sehr gut zur Durchführung einer *panel discussion*. Die Schülerinnen und Schüler erhalten als vorbereitende Hausaufgabe die gründliche Lektüre des Textes und die Bearbeitung der Aufgaben 1 und 2. Es ist denkbar, schon im Rahmen dieser Hausaufgabe eine Arbeitsteilung, d. h. die Unterteilung des Kurses in vier Gruppen (Karla, her parents, teachers, stationer) vorzunehmen. Im Unterricht sollten dann im Rahmen einer arbeitsteiligen Gruppenarbeitsphase zusätzliche Punkte für die unterschiedlichen Interessengruppen gesammelt und notiert werden, mit deren Hilfe später in einer kontroversen Diskussion stichhaltig argumentiert werden kann. Ferner bestimmt jede Gruppe ihre Vertreter für die Podiumsdiskussion. Abhängig von der Leistungsstärke des Kurses ist es ratsam, den Schülerinnen und Schülern *useful phrases* für die Diskussionsrunde an die Hand zu geben. Im Anschluss folgt eine Phase der Ergebnissicherung, die die tragfähigsten Argumente in gegenüberstellender Form unter der Fragestellung „Pencil Case With a Playboy Bunny Logo – Should It Be Banned by School?" zusammenführt.

Solutions

Activities p. 29

1. **Explain in a sentence or two a) Carla's view, b) her parents' view, c) the school's view, d) the stationer's view.**
   a) She liked the pink bunny with a bow tie (and was completely unaware of the Playboy connections).
   b) They thought it was wrong to make an issue of the logo, and that it was ridiculous to ban the pencil case. The school was responsible for bringing up 'adult' issues.
   c) Teachers regarded the bunny logo as inappropriate because of its links with Playboy magazine, so they banned the pencil case from the school.

d) The stationer said that the bunny logo was no longer closely associated with Playboy, and had become a popular fashion brand.

2. **Do you agree with the school or the parents – or can't you make up your mind? Talk about the problem and give reasons for your point of view.**
The arguments on both sides are set out above and in the text. Some useful expressions:
In my view ...,
I (don't) think ...,
Why on earth would anyone want to ...,
The teachers were overreacting, I'm on the parents/the teachers' side.
If a daughter of mine ...
On the other hand, we don't want to encourage ...
It's sneaky/underhand/dishonest of Playboy to put their logo on things for kids.

Upgrade-itis/Power Pestering Costs Parents a Cool £3bn

Texts and photographs

This material is intended to bring home to students the pressures on people in industrial countries to buy the latest products. From a parents' point of view, 'power pestering' from their children puts them under tremendous pressure to buy the latest or a more expensive model – and it applies to cars, houses and holidays as well as more traditional children's interests. As all the texts are relatively short and self-explanatory, no synopsis is provided for this material.

Unterrichtsempfehlungen

Eine ertragreiche Auseinandersetzung mit den Artikeln auf der Doppelseite (S. 30 und 31) erfordert eine vorbereitende Lektüre, die von den Schülerinnen und Schülern zu Hause geleistet werden sollte. Insbesondere die *pre-reading activity* auf S. 30 ist dabei zu berücksichtigen; die Lernenden sollten sich nach der Lektüre diesbezüglich Gedanken machen und nach Berührungspunkten zwischen den Artikeln und Aspekten, die an Werbestrategien erinnern, suchen. Die Verbindung zwischen den Bildern und Texten der Doppelseite und der Werbung könnte folgendermaßen formuliert werden:

It is of course the advertising industry which tells us about new products and makes us want to buy them. The main photo deliberately includes an early model mobile phone to show how quickly things change. Manufacturers who fail to update in time go to the wall (e.g. the British car industry, the German camera industry). The economies of rich countries would collapse if people stopped buying, buying, buying.
There is also a connection with globalisation here. If new economies in the far east can make very good products more cheaply than the established industrial countries, how will those countries maintain high salaries and low unemployment? The answer has to be via very high quality premium products and keeping ahead by means of innovation.

Die Aufgaben 1–3 auf Seite 32 können nach der in Stillarbeit vorgenommenen Lektüre im Rahmen eines Unterrichtsgespräches beantwortet werden. Dabei sollte von der Lehrkraft darauf geachtet werden, dass die Schülerinnen und Schüler aufeinander reagieren und unterschiedliche Beiträge nicht einfach isoliert für sich stehen bleiben. In leistungsschwachen Kursen muss vor der Beantwortung der Aufgaben an eine Sicherung des Textverständnisses gedacht werden.
Da die Aufgaben 4 und 5 sehr engen Lebensweltbezug aufweisen, können sie in Kleingruppen bearbeitet werden, wobei jede Gruppe ihre Ergebnisse in Form von kurzen

und prägnanten Statements dem Plenum vortragen sollte. Eine Fixierung dieser Statements auf Pappen ist wünschenswert. Die Lehrkraft kann Formulierungen vorgeben, z. B. indem sie die Aufgaben etwas umformuliert: *„To go on buying things is important and pleasing for us because ...“* Aufgabe 6 ist in Form einer schriftlichen Hausaufgabe zu erledigen.

Solutions

Activities p. 32

1. **What links the six small boxes and the man with the mobile?**
   (Note: although the word 'handy' is a nice English word – and appropriate for the object in question, it is not used for mobile phones in the English-speaking world.) Each of the boxes deals with a product which has undergone rapid updating from the time of its introduction. The man in the photo was obviously a smart youngish businessman using the latest 'must have' product of his day, but how we would laugh if someone used this model today.

2. **What is the significance of the photo below and the accompanying statistics?**
   They show the inevitable consequences of constant updating – huge quantities of waste. People throw away all kinds of goods just because they are no longer the latest model, even if they work perfectly or could easily be repaired.

3. **What role does "power-pestering" play?**
   Children are very good at putting pressure on their parents (power pestering), and parents are not very good at resisting it, even if they can ill-afford the products in question, especially when these are products from the adult world, which children have views on, too (cars, etc.). Parents want their children to be happy, and their happiness often appears to depend on possessing the 'right' brands and the latest products. So good parenting can easily become equated with buying your kids the 'right' stuff, rather than spending 'quality time' with them.

4. **Why is it important, and pleasing, for us all to go on buying things?**
   The economic argument was covered briefly above. We enjoy buying things because it is nice to have new things, impress our friends, be accepted as members of a group buying similar things, and also, in some cases, to have a better product. Sometimes the 'improvements' are unnecessary, e. g. in the case of ever larger numbers of pixels for digital cameras, or adding radios, MP3 players etc. to mobile phones.

5. **What is already happening as a result?**
   Various answers are possible:
   - Quite large numbers of people get into debt, particularly if they buy with credit cards.
   - We are not necessarily any happier when we have bought all this stuff.
   - Huge quantities of (electronic) waste are produced.
   - When consumers are in a buying mood, the economy booms.
   - People who cannot 'keep up' financially feel like second-class citizens, become depressed when they see all the beautiful, prosperous people in TV commercials, and may in some cases turn to crime.

6. **(Nearly) all of us want new and better things all the time, which is already leading to shortages of vital resources and environmental problems of all kinds, including global warming. Write a short essay in which you try to outline ways in which we can all enjoy the good life without wrecking the planet.**
   Some ideas:

- Trying to buy products which will not wear out/go out of date quickly
- Trying to reduce our 'carbon footprint' (the amount of energy in all forms used in our lives – everything from cheap flights to buying exotic fruits from the other side of the world to turning off equipment on standby, to encouraging parents to buy an economical car, to using public transport – or a bicycle)
- Public opinion is beginning to swing away from 'conspicuous consumption', so perhaps it is actually becoming fashionable to live economically.
- Recycling
- Try to define what 'the good life' means to you personally. How much does it really depend on possessing the 'right' brands and the latest products?
- Efforts in western Europe will have little effect while the Indian and Chinese economies in particular continue to grow so rapidly, but it makes sense (and sets a good example) to put our own house in order.

Cuttings

Synopses

Class war over a cup of coffee
Attempts are being made to persuade less wealthy and/or fashionable people to start buying coffee in more downmarket coffee shops.

Sexy Eidgenossen
A humorous Swiss video which has achieved cult status is intended to persuade women who are not interested in football to come to Switzerland during a World Championship. Athletic-looking, sexy Swiss men appear in the commercial, one of them topless. The commercial has upset some people, but The Swiss Tourist Board points out that women in bikinis have been used to advertise holiday destinations for years.

Getting on the brand wagon
Britain has not been very successful at establishing top brands such as Microsoft, L'Oreal etc. These brands have managed to make themselves part of international culture through hard work by managers over a long period, whereas in Britain the approach is not dedicated and long-term enough.

Turbo-consumerism
Nowadays a teenager from a middle-class family carries or wears a lot of expensive, desirable 'goodies', which makes him an obvious target for 'hoodies', who cannot afford to buy these status symbols.
A 'normal' person in the modern world is a successful consumer. Those without the 'must have' items of the day are failures. Poor people are falling further and further behind in this race. Keeping up is everything.

Companies go green in their ads
A number of leading companies from all kinds of fields are starting to stress the 'green' aspects of their products. Their reasons for doing so may be cosmetic, or they may really be starting to care about the environment.

The magic of spring
People drink huge quantities of bottled water nowadays, with over 200 brands competing for the market. A tiny company in Somerset has nevertheless managed to corner quite a large corner of the market. The secret of their success is a spring on their land. Hippies used to come and drink the water in the summer, claiming it had magic properties. This certainly helps to sell it, but the water also has remarkable properties from a purely scientific point of view.

Unterrichtsempfehlungen

Die aktuellen Textbeispiele auf den Seiten 33–36 beziehen sich auf vielfältige Bereiche der Produkt- und Werbelandschaft. Im Zusammenhang mit dem Aufgabenapparat eröffnet sich hier für die Lehrkraft die Chance, einen sehr individualisierten Unterrichtsprozess in Gang zu setzen. Die Lehrkraft sollte sehr gründlich den Aufgabenapparat vor dem Hintergrund der Stärken und Schwächen ihrer Lernenden in den Blick nehmen. Anschließend sollte sie die verschiedenen Teilaufgaben jeweils bestimmten Schülerinnen und Schülern zuordnen und diese in Arbeitsgemeinschaften zusammenführen.
Eine Bearbeitung der Teilaufgaben ist auf vielfältige Weise denkbar. Neben der Fixierung wichtiger Punkte und Antworten auf Lernplakaten und der Präsentation im Rahmen eines Galeriegangs, könnten Ergebnisse der Gruppen auf einer schuleigenen Lernplattform im Internet abgelegt werden. Im Rahmen einer Hausaufgabe ist es dann Aufgabe des gesamten Kurses, die Ergebnisse zu sichten, kritisch zu betrachten, zu ergänzen und natürlich zu würdigen. In einer folgenden Englischstunde sollte dann vor dem Hintergrund dieser Hausaufgabe eine Bewertung erfolgen.
In einer abschließenden Reflexion erhalten die Lernenden die Möglichkeit, zu benennen, was ihnen bei der Arbeit an den Teilaufgaben leicht- bzw. schwergefallen ist. Aus diesen Angaben sollte die Lehrerin/der Lehrer Schlüsse für die weitere Förderung der Lernenden und seine Unterrichtsarbeit ziehen.

Solutions

Activities p. 36

1. **Why are fast food restaurants offering new coffee brands?**
   Chains such as Starbucks have shown them that there is a big market for coffee, and they want their share of it.

2. **What market are they aiming at?**
   A more working class market than the customers who go to Starbucks etc.

3. **Why mention 'three easy-to-say sizes'?**
   Two reasons: They want to distance themselves from the very large – some would say ridiculous – range of coffees available in the up-market bars.
   They also want to appeal to customers who like simple choices/are less well-educated/don't like or are confused by the range in the up-market coffee bars.

4. **Explain this text to someone who doesn't speak German. (Don't forget to explain *Eidgenossen*!)**
   (See the synopsis.)
   Eidgenossen: Swiss citizens, literally people bound together by an oath (which was sworn in 1315).

5. **Why exactly do you think this video was so popular?**
   Some ideas:
   – ironic, humorous
   – sexy
   – may really have appealed to 'football widows'
   – possibly not what one expects from Switzerland
   – easily made its way round the world via the Internet

6. **Is it sexist as well as sexy?**
   Anything which shows one sex or the other without many clothes on is likely to offend people who set themselves up as guardians of public morals. In this case, the spot is so obviously intended to be humorous that the charge of sexism would be hard to defend.

7. **What exactly is the author complaining about?**
   He feels that Britain is poor at establishing top world-wide brands.

8. **What German brands would you expect to be well-known worldwide? What reasons can you think of for their success?**
   e.g. Mercedes (quality, prestige, tradition, long history as a top brand, instantly recognizable radiator grill)
   Nivea (blue tin, quality, reasonable price, wide range of cosmetic products linked to the original cream)

9. **Explain how Will Hutton thinks a company should go about establishing a top brand name.**
   It should try to ensure that the name of the company is seen as part of the national or international culture, and then work hard over the long term to keep it there (quality, advertising, public relations).

10. **What happened to the author's son – and why does his father think it couldn't have happened to him?**
    His son was mugged and had his iPod stolen. This couldn't have happened to the author when he was young because he didn't possess anything worth stealing.

11. **Explain Baumann's definitions of 'normal' and 'abnormal'. How far do you agree with him?**
    In Baumann's view, a 'normal' person is a successful consumer who can afford all the 'right' accessories. An 'abnormal' person is anyone who can't afford these items.
    Students will probably want to talk about:
    - pressure they may feel to wear the 'right' clothes and buy the 'right' accessories
    - whether it is fair to look down on students who can't afford to 'compete' in this way
    - 'mobbing' of people who fail to fit in
    - whether we mainly judge people nowadays in materialistic terms, and if so, if this is wrong – even disgraceful, or just a consequence of the kind of world we live in

12. **Why, according to the author, is this a bad time to be poor (in industrial countries)?**
    Keeping up with other fairly wealthy consumers has never been so important, because new desirable 'goodies' are produced at ever shorter intervals. People who can't compete fall further and further behind in this 'race' and may become depressed – or turn to crime in order to get what they also want, but can't buy.

13. **Why is 'green marketing' popular?**
    Because the environment has become a very big issue (fears of pollution, global warming, dwindling fossil energy sources etc). So advertisers inevitably want to persuade consumers that the products they are trying to sell are environmentally acceptable.

14. **What do you make of the company called Pet Ecology, its product names and its slogan?**
    Possible reactions:
    - totally cynical
    - sickening
    - blinding people with science
    - very clever – pet owners are vulnerable where their pets are concerned
    - no guarantee that their claims are true

15. **Just 'cosmetics' or something deeper? Find some examples of 'green' advertising and comment on them.**
(Individual student project-type work involving research analysis and personal comments)

16. **What exactly is the 'magic' element in Tufa Pure?**
It has a perfect energy profile (whatever this means!) according to dowsing tests.

17. **How about its more scientific qualities?**
It has a very high calcium content.

18. **Why do you think this brand of bottled water is such a success?**
Some reasons:
– 'little guys' taking on the 'big guys'
– exclusive image
– thought to be specially pure
– the mineral content
– the mystical element

19. **Would you drink Tufa Pure? Give reasons for your answer?**
(Personal statements)

When Don't Smoke Means Do

Text The author of this (anonymous) leading article points out that a clever 'anti-smoking' campaign sponsored by a tobacco company is actually intended to be ineffective.

Synopsis The Philip Morris tobacco company seems to be acting like a good citizen. It has sponsored television spots urging parents to warn their children about the dangers of smoking, and has also targeted young people directly. This kind of behaviour appears to be against the company's interests, since their prosperity depends on recruiting new smokers as the older ones die off. However, a study carried out by respected researchers concludes that the ads aimed at young people had no effect, while those aimed at parents might actually be counterproductive. When parents tell their children not to smoke, it is likely to make them feel more like lighting up. The real reason for these campaigns is to head off a government crackdown on smoking. If Philip Morris really wanted to stop people smoking, it would have to stress the deadly and addictive aspects of smoking, but it has done nothing of the kind.

Unterrichtsempfehlungen

Eine genaue Lektüre des Textes sollte vom Kurs geleistet werden. Da der Text nicht zu lang und für einen Oberstufenkurs einen angemessenen Steilheitsgrat aufweist, kann dies zu Beginn einer Unterrichtsstunde im Rahmen einer Stillarbeitsphase vorgenommen werden. Die ersten 3 Fragen des Aufgabenapparates sollten sich dann anschließen, da sie der Sicherung des Textverständnisses dienen und zu der kritischen Auseinandersetzung hinleiten, die durch die verbleibenden 3 Aufgaben initiiert wird. Es empfiehlt sich, die Aufgaben 4, 5 und 6 von jeder Schülerin und jedem Schüler in Einzelarbeit beantworten bzw. reflektieren zu lassen. Danach sollte ein intensiver dialogischer Austausch im Plenum angeregt werden.

Solutions

Activities p. 38

1. **Describe recent advertising activities by Philip Morris.**
   (See the first part of the synopsis above.)

2. **How do these activities *seem* to be counter-productive for a tobacco company?**
   At first sight, it would seem that spending a lot of money on anti-smoking campaigns would harm the company responsible by reducing their tobacco sales.

3. **How is it that the effect of this kind of advertising turns out to be negligible – or even has the reverse effect?**
   Points that could be made:
   – Teenagers often rebel against their parents, so a campaign which tells parents to warn their children about the dangers of tobacco is unlikely to be effective.
   – The ads aimed directly at teenagers were 'fuzzy-warm', so they might create favourable attitudes towards the tobacco company even if the message was "Think. Don't Smoke".
   – The really unpleasant aspects of smoking (disease, addiction etc.) were not stressed.

4. **How does the cartoon reinforce this effect?**
   The smokers in the cartoon are obviously enjoying their cigarettes – probably in (or outside as smoking bans in cafés are widespread) a fashionable café. We can see that they are happy, friendly, good-looking people, the sort of people we see in advertisements. So the unwritten message is "smoking is a desirable, socially acceptable, cool activity". The written message says the exact opposite. There is a saying, "A picture says more than a thousand words."

5. **What is the *real* motive behind Philip Morris's advertising?**
   The company hopes that this kind of advertising will convince the government that a crackdown on smoking (which would *really* hit tobacco sales) is not necessary.

6. **Make some notes about your own attitude to the whole business of smoking (image, advertising, addictiveness, health, bans in public places) and discuss the issue in class.**
   Points that could be made:
   – Most teenagers try smoking cigarettes at some point.
   – It counts as an 'adult', even cool thing to do at that age.
   – This image is reinforced by clever, extremely professional tobacco advertising in cinemas, on posters and in other places where it is still allowed.
   – The addiction is extremely hard to break – most people fail to give up, therapies often don't work, massive willpower required.
   – Perhaps a majority of smokers would give up if they could.
   – It's expensive.
   – Smokers claim to have the right to enjoy a cigarette in restaurants etc.
   – They tend not to accept that non-smokers have the right to a smoke-free meal, office environment etc.
   – Passive smoking is an important issue.
   – There are huge health issues in addition to lung cancer – nearly half of all smokers die early as a result of smoke-related illness.

And Finally ...

Unterrichtsempfehlungen

Die Schülerinnen und Schüler können am Ende des Kapitels ihre Kompetenzerweiterung in Bezug auf den Bereich „Advertising" unter Beweis stellen. In arbeitsteiligen Gruppen sollten sie nicht nur ihre kommunikative Kompetenz durch neu erworbene sprachliche Mittel zum Thema anwenden, sondern auch ihren Zuwachs im Bereich der interkulturellen und methodischen Kompetenzen berücksichtigen. Eine Vorplanung zusammen mit dem Lehrer sollte daher die Schülerinnen und Schüler auf diesen Zusammenhang aufmerksam machen. Eine Rückschau auf das mithilfe des Kapitels „Advertising – Buy One, Get One Free" Erarbeitete ist daher als Hinführung zu den Activities „Analysing Advertisements", die klar einen Arbeitsprozess strukturieren, funktional. Je nach Ausstattung der Schule ist eine Ergebnispräsentation der Gruppen in Form von PowerPoint-Präsentationen empfehlenswert. Da auch schon in der Mittelstufe das Thema Werbung im Englischunterricht thematisiert wird, ist eine Einladung einer entsprechenden Mittelstufenklasse zu empfehlen. Es wird somit ein deutlicher Anwendungsbezug hergestellt, aber auch etwas mehr Zielspannung erzeugt, die die Lernenden zur Präsentation von ansprechenden Ergebnissen motiviert.

Worksheet 3

Harwich to Hook

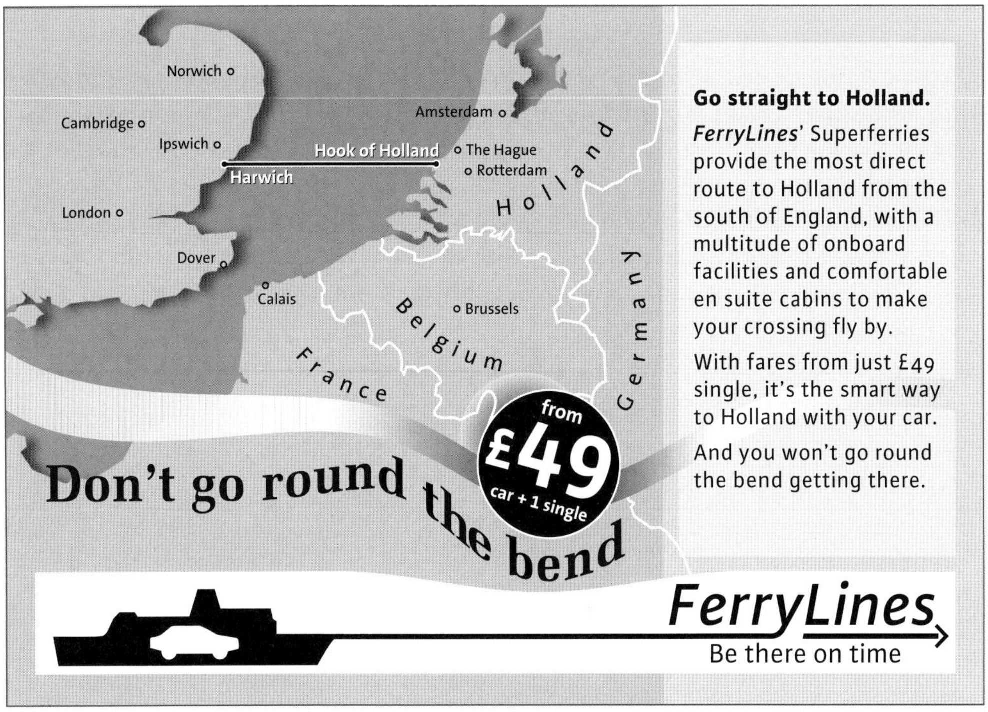

At first sight, this looks like a good offer, but as the Romans used to say, *caveat emptor* – let the buyer (of a ticket in this case) beware.
Several of the statements in the advertisement should make the buyer do just that – beware.

Activities

1. **Don't go round the bend**
   - **The expression has a second meaning as well as the obvious one – do you know what it is?**
   - **What *real* bend is referred to here? Does everyone have to go round it?**
2. **Go straight to Holland**
   - **Holland is a nice country – but is it a principal holiday destination for British people? Where will most of them be heading for?**
   - **Is Hook of Holland a good place to start from?**
3. **... the most direct route to Holland from the south of England**
   - **How do you get to Harwich from the south of England**
   - **What if you come from the north of England?**
4. **... from £49 car + 1 single**
   - **Are those 'comfortable en suite cabins' included in the price?**
   - **How many customers will actually pay that very low price?**
5. **... make your crossing fly by**
   - **Why does it need to 'fly by'?**
   - **How about crossing from Dover to Calais?**

Worksheet 3 Solution

1. **Don't go round the bend**
   - The second meaning is: don't go crazy.
   - It's not clear what *FerryLines* mean here – people travelling from the south of England to Dover have a more direct route to a ferry port – see also q.3.

2. **Go straight to Holland**
   - Holland is not a principal holiday destination for British people (except perhaps to see the bulb fields in the spring). Most of them head south to France, Spain etc.
   - If you are heading south, Hook of Holland is not a good place to start from. It involves a lot of extra miles compared with Calais.

3. **... the most direct route to Holland from the south of England**
   - This may be the only way to get to Harwich/Holland from the south of England (if we discount driving north from Calais) but you have to get round London via the infamous M 25, or make a huge detour to the north. So 'most direct' has to be taken with a pinch of salt.
   - It would actually be much more convenient to drive to Harwich from the north. Presumably FerryLines are trying to persuade more people from the south to travel with them.

4. **... from £49 car + 1 single**
   - A cabin is not included in the price, and on night sailings you have to book one.
   - A typical normal price in August 2008 was £149 for a single crossing, car + driver only.

5. **... make your crossing fly by**
   - The crossing needs to 'fly by' because it actually takes at least six hours.

Additional Activities

- **Students might like to try and create a more honest advertisement, bit one which would still persuade plenty of people to book with *FerryLines*.**
- **They could also write an angry letter to the shipping line from a customer who fell for the £49 offer and found it didn't apply to him/her.**

Computers and the Internet – Whatever Next?

Vorbemerkungen zum Kapitel

Das Kapitel enthält viele Texte, Fotografien und Bilder, die eine spannende und vielfältige Auseinandersetzung mit den nahezu unbegrenzten Möglichkeiten von Computer und Internet eröffnen. Es hat eine immer schneller vor sich gehende, fast schon dramatische Entwicklung in diesem Bereich eingesetzt; das Kapitel verschafft den Lernenden in sehr lebensweltnaher Form einen komprimierten Überblick und ermöglicht eine kritische und differenzierte Wahrnehmung hinsichtlich der Fragestellung des Kapitels „Computers and the Internet – Whatever Next?". Dabei werden sowohl bedenkliche als auch hoffnungsvoll stimmende Aspekte in den Blick genommen. Ferner ermöglichen Aufgabenapparate eine gezielte Vorbereitung der Schülerinnen und Schüler auf Operatoren und Aufgabenstellung, wie sie im Zentralabitur, insbesondere in NRW, denkbar sind. Der Umgang mit Sach- und Gebrauchstexten wird hier gezielt vertieft und gefördert.

Plug in and Play

Unterrichtsempfehlungen

Die Seite ist ideal, um die Schülerinnen und Schüler auf das Thema des Kapitels einzustimmen. Den Lernenden sollte Raum gegeben werden, spontan auf das Foto in der oberen Hälfte von Seite 40 zu reagieren und eine kurze Beschreibung zu geben. Zwei mögliche Punkte könnten sein:

- *Obviously humorous elements (cables, number of devices plugged in at the same time, fact that the screen is blank)*
- *Probably serious elements, too (most people now own several of the devices shown, dangers of being cut off from the 'real' world, risks of electro-magnetic pollution/health hazards)*

Die Beschreibung der Begriffe auf der unteren Hälfte führt fokussierter in die vielfältigen Teilbereiche des Kapitels ein und bietet einen funktionalen Sprechanlass:

virtual reality: *a world which seems realistic, but only exists in electronic form (likely to take on more and more realistic/bizarre elements as time goes on)*
Googling: *using the search engine Google (or other search engines) to find information about anything under the sun (already suffering from information overload – will have to become more user-friendly, but an essential tool in our world)*
the semantic web: *a vague term referring to the idea that using the web in future will be more like normal two-way communication between friends (see also "The Next Big Thing?", p. 44); the Internet is sure to become more and more two-way and user-friendly as time goes on, but some kind of major crash caused by overload/viruses etc. cannot be ruled out*
a participation culture: *the media will not just provide entertainment for passive recipients; the viewers/users will actively contribute (this is already happening on many websites and on reality TV – a reaction against the low quality of many contributions could help to bring back more traditional forms of entertainment.*
electronic books: *machines which (will) allow readers to download books and read them page by page on a screen by pressing a button (see also "Will We Close the Book on Books?", p. 43) may be the biggest change in reading habits since the invention of printing – or remain a minority thing – or a bit of both; people still buy CDs in spite of the iPod*

***Broadband**: fast internet access (likely to become faster still and cheaper)*

Der Lehrer sollte gerade in dieser Phase darauf achten, inwieweit den Schülerinnen und Schülern themenbezogenes Vokabular zur Verfügung steht und gegebenenfalls in den Folgestunden Vokabular und „useful phrases" bereitstellen. Das sukzessive Erarbeiten einer Vokabelliste/eines themenbezogenen Wortschatzes auf der Grundlage des Kapitels ist ebenfalls zu empfehlen. Daran anschließend erscheint es sinnvoll, die *pre-reading activity* zum Text auf Seite 41 zu besprechen und zu diskutieren. Unter anderem sind folgende Antworten denkbar:

- *'electronic' methods referred to in the text*
- *pages with prepared answers concealed in dictionaries if allowed or elsewhere*
- *notes on small pieces of paper in pencil case*
- *formulae stored on pocket calculator*
- *use 'toilet' break to phone friends, consult textbooks/notes etc.*
- *copy neighbour's work if seated near enough*

Mit der durch Seite 40 vorgenommenen Hinführung kann damit eine Einzelstunde abgeschlossen werden. Die gründliche Lektüre des Textes „Cheaters at College Shift to Higher Tech" erfolgt als Hausaufgabe.

Cheaters at College Shift to Higher Tech

Jonathan D. Glater

Text This text deals with a controversial topic on both sides of the Atlantic. It covers modern ways of cheating, and also takes a look at the (im)morality of using 'outside help' of whatever kind.

Synopsis Students have started to use all kinds of 'illegal' electronic means to improve their examination results. College officials have to try and find new ways to outwit the new generation of cheats. They ban Internet links to laptops and collect mobile phones before tests, for example. In some cases tests have to be written in the traditional way with pen and paper, which students accustomed to typing on a computer find difficult. Some cheats are so obsessed by the need to do well that they lose sight of the fact that they are doing wrong. Up to two thirds of students admit cheating. It seems that students are under more pressure to succeed than in the past. The pressure to obtain good results by any means is greater nowadays, and there is less strength of character among students to resist the temptation to cheat. College officials are being worn out by the battle to keep students honest. An iPod with a wireless earpiece would be very hard to detect. One simple but effective method of preventing cheating was to arrange desks with the students facing away from the invigilator, so that he could see their computer screens.

Unterrichtsempfehlungen

Die Unterrichtsarbeit erfolgt auf der Grundlage einer zuvor zu Hause geleisteten Lektüre des Textes. Für die Bearbeitung des gesamten Aufgabenapparates sollten 2–3 Unterrichtsstunden eingeplant werden. Sollte sich die Lehrkraft für die unten empfohlene Diskussion mit verteilten Rollen entscheiden, ist von 3 Unterrichtsstunden auszugehen.
Aufgaben 1 und 2 können in einer frontal ausgerichteten Unterrichtsphase erarbeitet werden, in der ein Tafelbild mit den zentralen Punkten entstehen sollte. Die Visualisie-

rung an der Tafel ergibt sich durch die Arbeitsanweisungen in den beiden Aufgaben. Für die Aufgaben 3–5 ist eine Bearbeitung in kleinen Gruppen von maximal 4 Schülern denkbar. Hier sollten die Schülerinnen und Schüler im Sinne einer *discussion group* mögliche Lösungsansätze diskutieren und sich auf gemeinsame Ergebnisse bzw. von allen getragenen Antworten einigen und in einen anschließenden Austausch mit anderen Gruppen treten – was die Bildung von neuen, größeren Gruppen impliziert.
Eine kontroverse Diskussion könnte durch Aufgabe 6 angeregt werden, insbesondere dann, wenn verschiedene Rollen verteilt werden und vorher etwas Zeit gegeben wird, sich auf verschiedene Rollen (z. B. Eltern, Schüler, Lehrer, Politiker/Schulministerin, Vertreter/in aus der Industrie, ein Universitätsprofessor ...) durch überzeugende bzw. provokante Argumente und Positionen vorzubereiten. Ein Resümee sollte die Diskussion, nachdem sich alle wieder aus ihren Rollen begeben haben, abschließen. Die abschließende Aufgabe des Aufgabenapparates (Nr. 7) sollte in Form einer schriftlichen Stellungnahme geleistet werden.

Solutions

Activities p. 42

1. **What new methods for cheating in examinations and other kinds of written work are described in the text. Note them down on the left of your page.**

2. **How are the authorities trying to stop cheating taking place? Add the strategies used on the right**

– notes loaded onto e-mail device	– (ban device from exam room – not specifically mentioned)
– spell check used during spelling test	– (de-activate spell check – not specifically mentioned)
– test questions photographed and transmitted to friends who sent back answers via SMS	– new proctoring (supervision) system (but students replying from their own rooms would be hard to detect, better to confiscate the phones)
– getting information from the Internet	– cut off Internet links/ban laptops/reintroduce traditional handwritten exams/arrange desks so that the invigilator can see computer screens
– using other people's essays etc. downloaded from the Internet	– no solution suggested (very hard to detect unless there are major differences (style, knowledge) between the student's previous work and the paper in question – even then very hard to prove); websites are being developed which will help teachers to detect non-original material

3. **How have attitudes to cheating changed in the student community in the US?**
Students are under more pressure to do well in exams in order to qualify for graduate school/desirable jobs, and at the same time they are less concerned than in the past about the moral issue.

4. **How did people cheat in the past? How were they caught?**
See the answers to the pre-reading task. People were generally caught when the invigilator looked up unexpectedly or crept up on them from behind and saw the offending notes etc. in use. In some cases visits to the toilet are/were supervised.

5. **In what ways are modern methods of cheating more efficient?**
In theory friends can be sent photographs of the questions (and send back the answers from outside the exam room), infinite amounts of relevant information can be accessed from the Internet, personal notes can be read from an e-mail device or listened to via a wireless earpiece.

6. **Many people in the German education system accept that there will be some cheating in tests etc., and it is not always regarded as a very serious offence. Make some notes on your views and discuss them with your fellow-students.**
Some points which could be made:
– if everyone else is cheating, it could be considered stupid not to do so oneself
– cheating is dishonest/wrong/immoral
– cheating invalidates/distorts the examination results
– those who cheat are being unfair to those who don't/gain an unfair advantage
– possible dire consequences of getting caught (expelled from school, banned from taking future exams, sense of shame, parental reactions)
– some people are very bad at memory-based tasks under examination conditions
– 'need' to cheat in order to perform well even if they are well-prepared

7. **Could there be some cases where cheating is justified? If so, try to give examples.**
The view of the editors of this handbook is that cheating is never justified. However, a case could be made in favour of the last item above. And how about the following real-life example:
A long time ago one of the editors was doing his military service in Britain and was being trained as a shorthand writer. When it came to the final test, the supervisor read out the text at the correct speed, then put down the piece of paper with the text on it and walked out, saying something like, "This is how I passed – make a couple of mistakes or it will look a bit suspicious. I'll be back in ten minutes." Needless to say all eight candidates passed with flying colours.

Will We Close the Book on Books?

Stephen King

Author and text

There are brief biographical notes in the students' book. It is worth adding that readers who only know of Stephen King as an extremely successful author of horror novels (and successful films based on them) are often not aware that he is a very thoughtful writer, with a particular interest in the whole craft of writing in general (see his book *On Writing: A Memoir of the Craft*).
Perhaps surprisingly for a writer with his reputation, King turns out to be a passionate defender of books new and old, in spite of or perhaps because of the possible threat to books from the Internet or other electronic media.

Synopsis

King sees booklovers as people who will stand up for books in spite of electronic threats to the printed page. People who read his own Internet-published novel would have preferred it in printed form. A new book is a pleasant object with an evocative smell, while an old book has the 'odor of history'. Non-literary people probably spend more time reading than they used to, but they will be reading websites, not books. This is sad, because books are perfect objects which need no batteries and never crash unless you throw them into the corner.

Unterrichtsempfehlungen

Die Lektüre des kurzen, jedoch sehr eindrücklichen Textes erfolgt im Plenum. Es ist empfehlenswert, den Text abschnittsweise von einzelnen Schülerinnen und Schülern laut vorlesen zu lassen. Im Anschluss sollte die Lehrkraft die Gelegenheit nutzen, gravierende Aussprachefehler zu korrigieren. Die ersten drei Aufgaben dienen der Sicherung des Textverständnisses. Die Liste (vgl. Aufgabe 1 und 2) könnte ohne großen Zeitaufwand von einzelnen Schülerinnen/einzelnen Schülern an der Tafel aufgeführt werden. Die 3. Aufgabe kann gemeinsam im Plenum beantwortet werden. Vor dem Hintergrund des Textes ist es ferner denkbar, die Lernenden nach ihren Lektüregewohnheiten zu fragen. Nach wie vor sind die Horror-Romane Kings und deren Verfilmungen bei Jugendlichen sehr beliebt. Die 4. Aufgabe bietet sich als schriftliche Hausaufgabe an und rundet den bis hier geleisteten Arbeitsprozess ab.
Eine Stellungnahme bezüglich des Themas „Will We Close the Book on Books?“ soll durch die letzte Arbeitsanweisung angeregt werden. Den Lernenden sollte hier in Form einer Stillarbeitsphase Gelegenheit gegeben werden, tragfähige Argumente für die eigene Position zu sammeln und zu strukturieren. Damit ist vor dieser Folie ein kontrovers geführtes Unterrichtsgespräch möglich.

Solutions

Activities p. 43

1. **Make a list of all the things Stephen King likes about printed books.**
   Books have weight and texture, feel nice in the hand, have a nice smell (acrid glue for new books, peppery for old books), old books have the smell of history, new books look like the future, books are a perfect medium needing no batteries, and they can't crash (in the electronic sense).
   (We could add: can be picked up and read on from the right page with the simple aid of a bookmark – any time, any place without having to be switched on, searched for on the hard disk etc., as long as there is some light)

2. **... and a list of he things he (and his readers) do not like about books on the computer screen.**
   – harder/less pleasant to read than from than a printed page, needs batteries (or mains electricity), can crash (text can get lost or be hard to find etc.), scrolling is hard on the eyes

3. **Why may 'non-bookworms' actually do more reading than they used to nowadays?**
   They may do quite a lot of reading as they surf the web.

4. **"No furniture so charming as books." How far do you agree? Write a paragraph in which you describe your own attitude to books, and also to other kinds of 'furniture' in your own room/home.**
   Students could mention favourite books they read when they were younger, books popular with their age-group at the moment, whether they ever read a book in English voluntarily, giving reasons in each case. Other kinds of 'furniture' could include posters, model aeroplanes, dolls and soft toys etc. left over from an earlier era, possible surviving colour schemes which seemed a good idea at the time, holiday souvenirs etc., not forgetting laptops, stereos, mobiles, MP3 players etc.

5. **It will soon be possible to buy a compact, lightweight electronic device which can be programmed with any book, newspaper or magazine ... What would the consequences be if this kind of device became popular – and would you want to buy one?**

Some points which could be made:
- we would almost certainly still have to pay for downloads
- no need for early morning newspaper deliveries
- very convenient to be able to download holiday reading, for example – only one item to pack
- would need batteries/mains adapter – how many hours of reading time available before new batteries or recharging become necessary?
- most readers enjoy buying a new book – would this pleasure now be lost – or will people go on buying books anyway (cf. the situation with CDs)?
- layout likely to be less interesting than in traditional magazines/newspapers
- harder to view whole newspaper pages
- nevertheless tremendously convenient/innovative etc., the long-term consequences could be truly dramatic

The Next Big Thing?

David Smith

Texts

The text on the left is a brief speculative view of present and possible future developments on the world-wide web. The short text on the right is a personal statement by Seth Godin, who has built a successful charity website – an example of what is possible.

Synopses

The Next Big Thing?
The main difference between the 'old' internet and 'Web 2.0' will be that it will include more networks and content generated by users. There are already more than 1,000 sites of this kind, including Wikipedia. The author believes that two-way communication of this kind is the modern equivalent of age-old person to person communication, and also gives us access to 'the wisdom of crowds'.

Seth Godin/Squidoo
Godin explains that his site enables people with ideas for helping people to put their ideas into practice. Squidoo helps them to build their own web pages which explain how their schemes would work, and provides the finance to get their schemes off the ground.

Unterrichtsempfehlungen

Der kurze Text „The Next Big Thing“ und das Zitat von Seth Godin können im Unterricht laut gelesen werden. Gravierende Aussprachefehler sollten von der Lehrkraft im Anschluss gebündelt aufgegriffen werden. An dieser Stelle sei einmal erwähnt, dass insbesondere die Aussprache eines korrekten „th“ vielen Schülerinnen und Schülern nach wie vor schwerfällt und die Aufmerksamkeit der Englischlehrerin/des Englischlehrers verlangt. Um insgesamt einen hohen Sprechanteil auf Seiten der Schülerinnen und Schüler zu erzielen, können die Aufgaben 1–5 mündlich in Kleingruppen beantwortet werden. Die Lehrkraft sollte dabei abwechselnd in die einzelnen Kleingruppen gehen und sich einen Eindruck über die kommunikative Kompetenz der Schülerinnen und Schüler verschaffen. Es sind besonders aus diesen Phasen des Unterrichts Maßnahmen zur individuellen Förderung der kommunikativen Kompetenz ableitbar.
Die letzte Aufgabe sollte als Abschluss der Unterrichtseinheit im Kurs diskutiert werden, dabei können sich die Schülerinnen und Schüler auf Aspekte aus den vorher erarbeiteten Antworten beziehen.

Solutions

Activities p. 44

1. **Explain the difference between a 'lean back' experience and a 'lean forward' experience, as these terms are used by the author.**
   A 'lean back' experience is a passive 'consumer' type of activity, whereas a 'lean forward' experience requires/allows/encourages the computer user to make an active/creative contribution him-/herself.

2. **What is supposed to be new about Web 2.0? How new does it seem to you?**
   Nowadays, there are all kinds of sites which are created or partly created by users, the most famous at the time of writing being Wikipedia and YouTube. However, students are sure to be able to add to this list.

3. **What does Squidoo do?**
   See the synopsis above.

4. **How far would you say that the kind of website described here marks a real step forward for users?**
   Most people would agree that two-way communication is basically a very good thing. However, it is already clear that the quality of content (for example on sites which publish home videos) is often terrible, and knowledge-based sites such as Wikipedia are vulnerable to having information tampered with and other kinds of abuse, so that their authority is compromised. However, the staff go to great lengths to weed out faulty material, and Wikipedia remains a tremendously useful website. Who is going to buy printed encyclopedias in the future (and dictionaries perhaps – although a dictionary in book form is a very convenient tool – see the Stephen King text on p. 43)?

5. **Is the 'new car' example a good case to choose?**
   Yes and no. It would be easy to consult several friends via the Internet, but there is no substitute for one really knowledgeable friend who comes with you to look at the car in question. On the other hand, it is possible to access all kinds of test reports on new and used cars via the Internet.

6. **Describe and discuss your own experiences with 'lean forward' websites.**
   Some points which could be made:
   – (older) men trying to seduce young girls via the Internet
   – problems with trying to make a personal contribution
   – privacy/exhibitionist issues
   – too much unstructured material
   – software problems

Campuses Connect Students Online

Janet Kornblum

About the text

The text explains that student-produced university websites are very successful in helping new students in particular to find their feet before and during their first term. These sites complement the official university websites and are actively recommended by the university authorities.

Synopsis

Freshmen at a typical American college feel much less nervous about life in college after having their questions about accommodation, student government and other issues likely to worry them answered by students further along the course. Administrators believe that nearly every college will soon have a website of this kind, because this is a familiar mode of communication for modern teenagers. Administrators use these sites along with the official university sites to market their institutions and also put freshmen at their ease. Some sites are just message boards, but others offer a full service including student profiles and two-way student-student communication. Where such sites exist, nearly all students use them. Administrators worry about some of the material which appears, but whenever possible they do not interfere because they can see how valuable these websites are.

Unterrichtsempfehlungen

Die *pre-reading activity* lädt zu einem offenen Unterrichtsgespräch ein, bei dem die Schülerinnen und Schüler ihre eigenen Erfahrungen und Gewohnheiten in Bezug auf ihre Nutzung des Internets und den kommunikativen Möglichkeiten, die daraus resultieren, einbringen können. Eine alternative Hinführung könnte durch den Lehrer gestaltet werden, indem er in der Unterrichtsvorbereitung gesichtete Schulseiten aus dem angloamerikanischen Raum von den Schülerinnen und Schülern in einem Teil einer Unterrichtsstunde unter einer bestimmten Themenstellung im Computerraum der Schule wahrnehmen lässt (beispielsweise: *Do you like the site? Why? How does the site connect students? Does it connect students?*). Auf diese Weise gelingt es, zielsprachliche Kultur direkt und zeitnah in den Klassenraum zu bringen. Im Anschluss an diese Arbeit fügt sich die Arbeit an dem ersten Teil des Aufgabenapparates schlüssig an. Aufgabe 1 a) sollte zügig im Plenum bearbeitet werden; Aufgabe 1 b) hingegen wird vor der Auswertung im Plenum im Rahmen einer Partnerarbeit gelöst. Es ist zu empfehlen, die zentralen Ergebnisse an der Tafel unter der Leitfrage „Why has social networking become important for schools and students?“ zu sichern. Aufgabe 1 c) dient der inhaltlichen Vertiefung und dem Aufbau von Schreibroutine. Sie sollte als Hausaufgabe bearbeitet werden.
Die verbleibenden Aufgaben bieten Sprechanlässe und laden zu Unterrichtsgespräch und Diskussion ein. Vor der Arbeit an der Aufgabe 3 a). kann der Lehrer je nach Bedarf seines Kurses die Gelegenheit nutzen und Techniken zur Bildbeschreibung wiederholen.

Solutions

Activities p. 46

1. a) Why are more and more schools creating their own sites?
b) With a partner go through the text again and list important points and details which show why social networking has become important for schools and students.
c) Write a summary of the article focusing on the main aspects.

a) They do because these sites enable students to find out what they really want to know about the institution they attend or are about to join. They believe that information from other students is likely to be more reliable than ‘official’ information on some issues, and they like being able to communicate with other students on a two-way basis.

b) Important points:
- Colleges in America are setting up private websites run by students.
- Freshmen can ask senior students about anything that worries them about going to college.
- Nearly all colleges will soon have websites of this kind because they are so popular and useful.
- Students are familiar with communicating in this way.
- The sites are used by administrators, too, for marketing their institution and to provide help for students.

- Some sites are very basic, but others provide a wide range of services.
- Nearly all students use these sites when they are available.
- Administrators are sometimes worried about material on the sites, but they avoid censorship whenever possible.

c) See the synopsis above.

2. **Michael Bugeja of Iowa State University mentions that some administrators worry that online networks could create legal problems. What kind of problems? Give examples and explain.**
   Some potential problems which could have legal implications:
   - insulting information on the site about college staff or other students
   - intimate details of students' and lecturers' private lives appearing on the site
   - dangerous/damaging rumours could circulate
   - inaccurate or deliberately misleading information about the institution
   - the site could be used for mobbing unpopular students/lecturers
   - the site could be invaded by unscrupulous criminals of various kinds including sexual abusers

3. **a) In pairs describe the drawing and take notes.**
   b) Does it support the idea that there is "a generation that socialises online on websites"? Give reasons.
   a) The drawing shows two students, one male, one female, sitting at their laptops and typing on the keyboards. We cannot see what is shown on the screens, but the cables leading from the two computers form hands which are reaching out towards one another – an obvious symbol for communication/an offer of help/friendship.
   b) The drawing clearly supports the idea that (young) people naturally communicate with one another electronically, via their laptops (and of course their mobile phones). (Some parents and educators naturally worry that this kind of communication could be less healthy/natural etc. than actually talking to friends on a face to face basis. On the other hand, there is no doubt that people keep in touch better via the Internet than they ever did via 'snail mail'.)

The World Is Not Enough

Rob Waugh

Text

The text describes a virtual world accessed via computers in which it is possible to buy and sell goods and property, and move around in the form of your virtual persona or 'avatar' (a better word, which is not used in this article).

Synopsis

The article begins with the dramatic information that a virtual Adidas shoe took 1000 hours to create, but sells for 10p in the virtual world game called Second Life. People who participate can use their keyboards to move around this virtual world. There are shops where they can buy clothes, cars and mobile phones using the Second Life currency, Linden Dollars, which have to be bought with real money, more and more of which is being spent on this game. Major players such as the BBC and pop groups arrange virtual concerts. A part-time teacher has become the most successful virtual estate agent. More than 1,000 people 'live' in houses which she has sold. Her virtual world job is beginning to take over from her real job. A few years ago no one imagined that virtual reality could become so real.

Unterrichtsempfehlungen

Der Umgang mit dem Text über die für Schülerinnen und Schüler sicherlich bekannte virtuelle Plattform „Second Life“ folgt dem Aufgabenapparat. Während durch die ersten 4 Fragen das Textverständnis gesichert wird, können die Schülerinnen und Schüler mit der 5. Aufgabe Position beziehen in Bezug auf ihre Interessen in einer virtuellen Welt wie „Second Life“. Vor diesem Hintergrund kann eine *informal debate* vorbereitet und durchgeführt werden (vgl. Aufgabe 6). Die Lehrerin/der Lehrer sollte ausreichend Zeit zur Verfügung stellen, damit die Lernenden stichhaltige Argumente und Begründungen für ihre persönlichen Sichtweisen sammeln können. Darüber hinaus empfiehlt sich, Regeln für eine *debate* zu wiederholen und den Schülerinnen und Schülern *discussion gambits* an die Hand zu geben. Sie sollten nachhaltig dazu aufgefordert werden, diese im Rahmen der *debate* zu verwenden.

Die den Aufgabenapparat abschließende Aufgabe 7 ermöglicht eine sehr kreative Auseinandersetzung mit dem Thema. Die Schülerinnen und Schüler sollten zunächst ihre virtuelle Welt in einer Hausaufgabe entwerfen und später dem Plenum in Form eines kurzen, gut strukturierten Vortrages präsentieren. Es ist denkbar, dass Schülerinnen und Schüler die Aufgabe mithilfe ihres Computers lösen und im Computerraum der Schule dem Plenum vorstellen. Besonders gelungene Entwürfe könnten auf der Homepage der Schule veröffentlicht werden.

Solutions

Activities p. 48

1. **What can you buy in Second Life?**
   trainers, land, houses, clothes, cars, pets ...

2. **How does it differ from typical computer games?**
   It is focused on creativity – or acquiring things designed by other people – in order to be able to 'live' a second life on the website. There is no violence or goal-orientation of the kind associated with typical videogames.

3. **How are people making money from Second Life?**
   They design and/or buy and sell things in the virtual world which has its own currency, Linden Dollars. These dollars can be bought and sold using real money.

4. **How do you 'play'?**
   You buy and install the software, then you equip yourself with a virtual persona or avatar so that you can move around using your keyboard, meet other virtual people, buy consumer goods in virtual shops, and even acquire a virtual house on virtual land for you to 'live' in.

5. **There must be more to it than buying property etc. What else could Second Lifers do? If you signed on, what would you be interested in doing?**
   Some ideas:
   - meeting other virtual people/dating
   - exploring the virtual world – driving around in a virtual car or on a virtual Harley Davidson
   - thinking of a business plan to make some money yourself
   - offering services which other people have not thought of yet
   - designing a really attractive persona/avatar for yourself
   - wearing/doing things which you would never dare to wear/do in the real world

6. **There is a science fiction story in which people acting in a virtual environment eventually die, slumped in front of their computer screens [...]. Do you see this kind of danger [...] with websites like Second Life?**
Some points for and against taking part in this kind of activity:

for	**against**
– could be very entertaining/exciting/creative	– danger of addiction
– an escape from a dull life	– for someone with a dull life, it could be difficult to return to reality
– business opportunities	– some people might more or less stop making any effort in the real world
– for some (possibly unemployed) people a virtual world could provide a real job/income	– there is a kind of deception involved – users are fooling themselves
– a chance to try out different life styles	– you might spend a lot of real money on virtual goods
– you can be more daring/attractive/successful than in the real world	

7. **What would *your* 'Second World' be like? Design your ideal virtual environment and present it to your class, with graphics if possible.**
(free creative activity)

Worksheet 4

A Survey

Fill in the form below and discuss the results in class. Work together to produce a summary showing percentages etc., then write a short essay with the title: "What computers and the Internet mean to our class."

1. For how many hours a week do you use a computer as a rule?	approximately ____________ hours
2. Try to decide roughly how much time you usually spend per week on the following activities:	– writing e-mails: ____________ – general surfing: ____________ – research for school work: ____________ – writing essays on the computer: ____________ – ebay/looking for things to buy: ____________ – teenage websites/chat rooms: ____________ – consulting online dictionaries or encyclopedias: ____________ – other (please specify): ____________ – games: ____________
3. Most people have problems with their computers from time to time. Describe typical problems you have encountered. Did you get angry, talk to the computer, attack it? How were the problems solved, if they were?	
4. Have you had any unpleasant experiences via your computer, e.g. identity theft, hate mail/electronic mobbing, correspondents with ulterior motives? Please give details.	
5. In what ways do you think computers/the Internet could be improved?	
6. If you are to some extent 'anti' computers, explain what you have against them. Do you agree with the view that computers are mainly 'a male thing'?	
7. How would your life/our lives change if there was some kind of mighty worldwide crash which put all computers out of action for several weeks or permanently?	

Films and TV – Wide Screens for Narrow Minds?

Vorbemerkungen zum Kapitel

Das Fernsehen hat sich zum kulturellen Leitmedium unserer Zeit entwickelt. Der Fernsehkonsum ist trotz der vielfältigen Möglichkeiten des Internets und verschiedener Computerspiele nicht gefallen. Es ist hingegen festzustellen, dass der Konsum von Medien insgesamt weiter gestiegen ist. Für die Schülerinnen und Schüler wird mit dem Kapitel in ganz erheblichem Maße ihre Alltagskultur aufgegriffen. Das Kapitel visiert u. a. an, einen Beitrag zu leisten, die Schülerinnen und Schüler dafür zu sensibilisieren, kritisch mit der medialen Repräsentation von Wirklichkeit umzugehen. Ferner wird die Rolle und die Zukunft des Kinos vor dem Hintergrund moderner Entwicklungen beleuchtet.

Cartoons

Unterrichtsempfehlungen

Die Vorgehensweise ergibt sich aus dem durch die Arbeitsanweisungen vorgegebenen Dreischritt und initiiert einen gruppendynamischen Arbeitsprozess. Sollte der Kurs wenig Erfahrung im Umgang mit Cartoons haben, empfiehlt sich ein kurzer Lehrervortrag vor Beginn der Gruppenarbeitsphase, der zentrale Elemente diesbezüglich wiederholt. Dabei ist evtl. auch an geeignetes Sprachmaterial zu denken, welches den Schülerinnen und Schülern dann auf Handouts zur Verfügung gestellt werden sollte. Ferner sollten die Schülerinnen und Schüler dazu angehalten werden, nicht nur auf die inhaltliche Tragkraft ihrer Antwort zu achten, sondern auch durch eine ansprechend beschriftete Folie und einen gut durchdachten, strukturierten Vortrag, die Aufmerksamkeit des Plenums zu sichern. Die Lehrkraft sollte daher auch Zeit zur Übung der Präsentationen innerhalb der Gruppen zur Verfügung stellen. Dafür kann den Oberstufenschülerinnen und Oberstufenschülern die Freiheit eingeräumt werden, die Präsentation außerhalb des gemeinsamen Kursraumes – auf dem Gang, in einem freien Klassenraum – für ein vorgegebenes Zeitfenster zu üben bzw. vorzubereiten.

Solutions

Activities p. 49

1. **Form five groups. Each group should work on one cartoon**
2. **Describe your cartoon and point out its message. How do the different elements of your cartoon (i. e. figures, captions and bubbles) highlight the message?**

No exit

This cartoon illustrates a choice of three TV channels, one showing luggage going round and round for ever on a carousel, one showing an endless traffic jam, and the third showing slow-moving clouds. The first two channels can be seen as the equivalent of 'moving wallpaper' – just something to watch mindlessly, while the third actually has a purpose – the slow-moving clouds are intended to help cure a hangover. The message is quite clear – see the subheading for the chapter

Mother reading book through TV screen

The cartoon shows a little boy sitting on a stool in front of a TV with an indoor type aerial which is standing on a low cupboard. His mother is standing behind the TV (which cannot have any works/inside/screen), and leaning forward so that her head and hands appear in the aperture where the screen would normally be. She is holding a book with the printed side towards her son, and pointing at the text/encouraging him to read. The message is that many modern children prefer sitting in front of a screen to reading a book. No doubt this is true, but the 'Harry Potter phenomenon' has in fact 'infected' a whole generation of children with the 'reading virus', so there is still hope!

You better not ...

The cartoon shows a 'father and son' situation. The father is reading a newspaper which has a headline saying that children watch too much TV, while the son is in fact watching a shooting on TV, sitting on a carpet/mat right in front of the screen. In the bubble, the father warns his son against becoming violent. The message is that parents who do nothing to stop their children watching violence on TV should not be surprised if their children become violent.

Note: This remains a controversial issue. Some experts claim that watching violence does not make people violent, others think it does. The degree of influence may be related to family background and other social factors. There is a fair amount of agreement that the senses become numbed to some extent when people watch a lot of violence on TV and videos.

Man sitting on armchair in ice-hockey goal

An overweight man is sitting in a comfortable armchair placed inside an ice-hockey goal, drinking beer from a can.

He is wearing a sports shirt, shorts, football-type socks and football boots. He has a glazed expression on his face. We can assume he is watching a sports programme on his TV. The message is that 'passive' sports is a sad/pointless/unhealthy activity unless it is accompanied by some 'active' sporting activity.

Cartoon in margin

This stark/disturbing/science fiction type cartoon shows a man in a dark overcoat who is holding his head in his right hand (his other hand is in his coat pocket). His head has been replaced by a TV set with an indoor aerial on the top. He is staring at the screen with a miserable/fixed/sad/obsessed expression on his face. The screen is blank. Various interpretations/messages are possible, e. g.

- TV is very bad for us
- the modern world is de-humanizing us
- the man is the victim of a terrible experiment
- it's just a drawing
- it's intended to start us thinking about the implications of watching too much TV, and should not be taken too seriously
- the blank screen could imply that there's nothing worth watching anyway

3. **Put down your findings on a transparency and present them to your class.**
   (Group work based on the above)

Amusing Ourselves to Death

Neil Postman

Author and text

Neil Postman is a highly respected expert in his field. In this short text he puts forward the idea that TV has persuaded us that entertainment 'is the natural format for all experience'. This is really another, easier to interpret way of saying 'the medium is the message' (Marshall McLuhan).

Synopsis

It does not mean very much to say that television is entertaining. Some of it probably is, and there is no reason why it should not be. However, television presents the world to us with a smiling face, however shocking the subject matter may be. The assumption is that whatever appears on our screens is there for our amusement. If this were not the case, newscasters would not invite us to 'join them tomorrow' after they have shown us enough violence to last us for a month of sleepless nights. Everything about a news show, the smiling, attractive presenters, the music, the commercials and so on, reinforces the idea that it is not to be taken seriously. It is solely a format for entertainment.

Unterrichtsempfehlungen

Beginnen kann man mit der Einstimmung auf den Text im Rahmen eines offenen Unterrichtsgespräches durch die *pre-reading task*.
Folgende Ergebnisse sind denkbar:

- *TV makes us mindless.*
- *Too much amusement/entertainment results in 'dumbing down'.*
- *A lot of what we call 'communication' is one way/pointless/about nothing of any importance whatsoever (cf. the Eurovision Song Contest, endless sports programmes, reality TV, mobile phone calls overheard, soap operas etc.).*
- *Students may be suspicious that Postman's arguments could be one-sided, and wish to defend some (kinds of) programmes on TV. They should be encouraged to talk about examples of 'good' television, and explain what they mean by it.*

Danach sollten die Schülerinnen und Schüler in einer Stillarbeitsphase/Einzelarbeit konzentriert die ersten beiden Aufgaben angehen. Während die erste Aufgabe eine gründliche Lektüre und eine gezielte Informationsentnahme verlangt, fordert die 2. Aufgabe, das Gelesene in Bezug zur eigenen Medienkultur zu setzen. Eine Ergebnissicherung bezüglich Aufgabe 1 sollte in einem Unterrichtsgespräch erfolgen, wobei die Lehrerin/der Lehrer die zentralen Argumente aus dem Text an der Tafel unter der Überschrift „Entertainment: supra – ideology?“ festhalten sollte. Ein weiterer Austausch vor dem Hintergrund der 2. Aufgabe kann ebenfalls in Form eines Unterrichtsgespräches erfolgen. Die Lehrkraft sollte im Anschluss überzeugende Punkte aus den Schülerbeiträgen in einem kurzen Vortrag bündeln und zusammenfassen.
Zur Bewältigung der letzten Aufgabe ist eine Zusammenarbeit mit der Fachschaft Musik, oder aber, falls existent, mit einer „Film AG“ zu denken, die über die erforderliche Ausrüstung verfügen. Erfahrungsgemäß verfügen unsere Schülerinnen und Schüler durch den Umgang mit Internetseiten wie z. B. YouTube oder MySpace über erhebliche Kompetenz zur Erstellung von kleinen Videoaufnahmen.

Solutions

Activities p. 50

1. **Neil Postman criticises the connection between entertainment and television. Outline his arguments.**
(See the synopsis above, apart from the first sentence.)

2. **Think of German news shows you watch. What role does entertainment play?**
Some students will be able to compare German news programmes with American news channels via satellite. They should be encouraged to do so.
Broadly speaking, the entertainment element is played down on German TV, but news of celebrities, football transfers, sports results etc. tends to be given as much prominence as 'real' news. The regional news services go much further in the entertainment direction (car crashes, interesting pets, rescues of all kinds, tourism topics, people doing interesting jobs ...). British TV includes human interest stories in the main news.
Note: While work on this book was in progress, an American news presenter refused to broadcast the release from prison of 'celebrity' party girl Paris Hilton as the first item on her news programme – this could just possibly indicate that a change of heart may be on the way.

3. **In groups of 4 or 5 collect the latest news at your school in your town etc. and stage your own news show. Record it on video and present it on TV to your class or other groups at your school**
(Individual project work – a really good video could be shown at a parents' evening.)

Additional activity

4. **a) Imagine a news show with (plenty of) entertainment. What would it look like? Present your ideas to your class.**
There obviously is a degree of entertainment in the German TV news anyway, so students should be encouraged to come up with exaggerated news stories perhaps one news item per student. Some ideas:
   - a politician presenting a speech in the form of an operatic aria with lots of gestures etc.
   - 'suitable' jingles/signature tunes each time a particular presenter/politician/TV personality appears on the screen
   - tasteless 'funny' presentation of famine/disasters etc.
   - caricatures of anyone famous
   - use of tones of voice/camera work/choice of vocabulary to make people or news items seem funny/entertaining/ridiculous

   b) Discuss if there would be an audience for such a news show.
There are already satirical versions of the news on radio and TV, so we can be sure there would be an audience for this kind of news, but not as a replacement for the 'serious' news – although it has to be said that the standard German news programme is often rather boring (obscure political issues, whether top people are going to keep or lose their jobs, problems with the unions ...), so a little brightening up would not come amiss.

I Want to Be On TV

Green Day

Song

This song is an ironical comment on the tremendous urge some people feel to become famous by being on TV (cf. the Big Brother phenomenon), whatever the consequences, and however empty or destructive (drug/alcohol addiction etc.) success turns out to be.

Synopsis

The speaker/singer wants to be attractive enough to appear on various kinds of TV show so that people will know him and stare at him in the street. He is prepared to do anything to become famous. He thinks this will get him reported on in magazines, give him access to free drugs and expensive, fashionable clothes. This life-style would make the world 'all mine'.

Unterrichtsempfehlungen

Die *pre-reading activity* könnte alternativ zur im Buch vorgeschlagenen Partnerarbeitsphase auch dadurch angegangen werden, dass der Lehrer die Satzanfänge *I want to be on TV because ... – I don't want to be on TV because ...* auf jeweils ein großes Plakat schreibt und die Schülerinnen und Schüler bittet, nacheinander einen Satzanfang zu wählen und fortzuführen. Im Plenum können dann die Aussagen kommentiert und eine erste Orientierung in Bezug auf den Songtext erzielt werden. Denkbare Antworten sind:

positive
- *because I would like to be well-known/would like people to recognize me in the street*
- *because the pay is supposed to be very good*
- *because it would be a very interesting/demanding/exciting kind of job*
- *because I would like to work with people on TV who I like and respect*
- *because a 'nine to five' kind of job just doesn't appeal to me*
- *because television is the prime medium of our age – this is 'where it's all happening'*
- *because I want to study journalism, and that would be a good preparation for a job in television*

negative
- *because I'm not a publicity-seeking, very self-confident sort of person*
- *because I don't watch much TV and don't see the point of a job in the television industry*
- *because I would hate to be pursued by the paparazzi/I want to keep my private life private*
- *because I already have other career plans which I hope will suit me better*
- *because it is very hard to get into television, and I don't think I would have much chance without good connections*

Die Aufgaben 1 und 3 sollten in Einzelarbeit/in einer Stillarbeitsphase bearbeitet werden. Anschließend sollten einzelne Ergebnisse/Textproduktionen dem Plenum präsentiert und die Möglichkeit zur Kommentierung eingeräumt werden. Die zweite Aufgabe kann in einem offenen Unterrichtsgespräch diskutiert werden. Die Lehrkraft sollte dabei die Schülerinnen und Schüler dazu anhalten, ihre Begründungen anhand des Textes zu illustrieren. Danach sollte der Song vorgespielt werden, z. B. bei „YouTube", um zu der „Karaoke Competition" hinzuführen.
Die „Karaoke Competition" kann auf der einen Seite natürlich mithilfe des Musiklehrers bearbeitet werden. Darüber hinaus bieten sich im Internet viele kostenlose Möglichkeiten, mit einfachen Mitteln eine „Karaoke Version" zu erstellen.
Vielleicht gibt es an der Schule sogar eine Rockband, die bereit wäre, im Rahmen eines Schulkonzertes die Versionen der Schülerinnen und Schüler zu präsentieren.

Solutions

Activities p. 51

1. **What is the song about? Write one or two sentences.**
   See *About the song* and the synopsis above.

2. **Analyse the singer's attitude towards TV. Does he really want to be on TV? Give reasons.**
   He does not really want to be on TV (at least, in this mode/persona – a singer presumably wants to become famous in real life). The repetition of 'desirable' kinds of programme to be on without any reasons shows that the wish has no real substance behind it, cf. the 'famous for being famous' syndrome referred to in the first chapter.
   The actual 'benefits' referred to in the fifth verse are questionable, to say the least, and the song ends with the repeated bald statement 'I wanna be on TV', making it clear that the speaker has no reason other than the wish to be famous.

3. **Following the pattern of the song add one more verse and read it to your class.**
   Individual creative work. Students could be encouraged to start lines with 'wanna' and/or 'gonna' to give their work an authentic flavour.

4. **With the help of your music teacher make a Karaoke version of the song. Sing your version to your class. Who is the best? Take a vote.**
   Individual creative work

57 Channels (And Nothin' On)

Bruce Springsteen

Singer Bruce Springsteen was born in 1949. He can be seen as the legitimate heir to all-time greats such as Elvis and Bob Dylan. His own brand of 'heartland rock' is often centred around his native New Jersey. His songs often deal with men and women struggling to make ends meet.

Synopsis The speaker has bought a bourgeois house in the Hollywood hills, and settles down to watch cable TV with his girlfriend. They surf all 57 channels but can't find anything worth watching. Next day he buys a satellite dish and connects it up but still can't find anything worth watching, so his girl friend leaves him. He goes out and buys a gun which he uses to blast his TV to pieces. As a result he is taken to court for disturbing the peace. His defence is 'Fifty-seven channels and nothin' on'. The judge concludes that he is close to madness.

Unterrichtsempfehlungen

Mithilfe der nachfolgend aufgeführten Sparten und Ausdrücke kann zunächst die *prereading activity* behandelt werden.

Kinds of programme:
news, current affairs, nature, documentary, comedy, sitcom (situational comedy), films, detective/police series, reality TV, sports, cartoons, children's programmes, regional programmes, educational programmes, consumer programmes, cooking/travel/fashion/celebrity programmes

Some useful expressions:
I'm really keen on ...
I can't stand ...
I know it's rubbish but I watch ... anyway
I wish there were more programmes like ...
I can't understand why anybody watches ...

Die ersten vier Aufgabentypen sind in Anlehnung an Aufgabenstellungen gestaltet wie sie ähnlich auch im Zentralabitur in NRW Verwendung finden. Vor der Bearbeitung der ersten Aufgabe bzw. nach der *pre-reading activity* kann der Song von Bruce Springsteen vorgespielt werden, wobei die Schülerinnen und Schüler den Text mitlesen. Besonders die Ergebnisse zur zweiten Aufgabe sollten an der Tafel gesichert werden. Die Schülerinnen und Schüler sollten darüber hinaus bei allen Aufgaben dazu angehalten werden, ihre Sichtweisen und Lösungsmöglichkeiten konkret anhand des Liedtextes zu belegen und Zeilen zu benennen.
Die Aufgabe 4 kann in schriftlicher Form als Hausaufgabe erledigt werden. Die Lehrerin/der Lehrer sollte später nach dem Zufallsprinzip einige Hausaufgaben auswählen und vorlesen lassen; dem Plenum kommt die Aufgabe zu, die Dialoge vor dem Hintergrund des Liedtextes zu bewerten. Es sollte die Frage im Zentrum stehen, ob die Dialoge sich schlüssig aus dem Liedtext ergeben bzw. ob Textsignale aufgegriffen wurden.
Für Aufgabe 5 muss eine Unterrichtsstunde eingeplant werden. Die Schülerinnen und Schüler erarbeiten ihre Ergebnisse in Gruppen. Besonders Aufgabe 5 b) kann zu einer abschließenden, kontroversen Diskussion im Plenum genutzt werden.

Solutions

Activities p. 52

1. **In pairs, divide this song into units reflecting the singer's situation.**
   - buys a TV with a cable connection and hopes to enjoy his viewing
   - finds there is nothing on
   - connects up satellite TV
   - still nothing on
   - girlfriend leaves
   - buys gun and wrecks the TV
   - taken to court for disturbing the peace

2. **"Fifty-seven channels and nothin' on" Why is this chorus repeated so often? What is its function?**
   Points which could be made:
   - wants to emphasise the fact that he can't find any good programmes
   - the repetition itself is boring like the programmes (but this doesn't make the song boring)
   - The number itself reminds listeners of 'Heinz 57 varieties'– where there may not be all that much variety either – otherwise the exact number does not matter. In fact, several hundred channels are available nowadays, but Springsteen's message is as valid as ever.

3. **a) Do you support the singer's chorus? Are there too many channels and nothing on?**
   (personal opinions)

   b) What seems to be the singer's real problem?
   Some ideas:
   - can't think of any other kind of entertainment
   - thinks this is the only way to keep a girlfriend

– has picked the 'wrong' kind of girlfriend
– has no alternative strategy when TV fails to interest him and his girlfriend, so he turns to violence
– he has a very narrow outlook generally

4. **Continue the dialogue between the judge and the singer.**
A suggestion:
Singer: I'm not mad, your honour, just driven crazy by poor quality TV.
Judge: Can't you think of any other way of spending your evenings?
Singer: Well no, your honour. What else is there?
Judge: It's not my job to answer questions like that.
Singer: What do ***you*** do in the evenings, judge?
Judge: That's none of your business.
Singer: So do I go to prison or not?
Judge: 57 days – and I think you'll find prison even more boring than TV.

5. **a) In groups, compare the cartoon to the song. What similarities or differences can you find? Take notes.**
Some points to make:
– The basic message is the same – TV/home media are the only form of entertainment for the characters.
– No characters visible in the cartoon – but we know they're in there. In the song the singer lays his feelings bare.
– The cartoon is clearly much more modern than the song because new media are available (blackberry, SMS, HDTV).
– The cartoon is generally much more extreme, much more of a caricature. In the song the singer only makes two attempts to get better entertainment, both via the TV screen.

b) Has progress improved the quality of entertainment? Give reasons.
Personal views which could include:
– The *quantity* of entertainment has grown exponentially.
– iPods etc. mean that you can take vast amounts of personally chosen music around with you and listen to it more or less anywhere.
– People can contribute to TV programmes, websites etc. themselves instead of consuming entertainment passively; potentially a good thing although the quality of most such material is an issue.
– Most people feel that a lot of popular entertainment is rubbish.
– However, there is also a good deal of *quality* entertainment available – not always as accessible as the vast amounts of poor quality material.
– Film techniques such as special effects, cartoons etc. have improved dramatically (this does not necessarily result in better quality generally).
– We don't have to watch material which we consider poor, boring, in bad taste, etc. We have a choice. We can look for better quality entertainment elsewhere on TV, or we can turn off the set.

Stupid girls

Pink

Singer and Song

Pink is a very successful American singer/songwriter in the rock tradition who has sold over 20 million albums. Birth name: Alecia Beth Moore.
In this song Pink alternates between criticising the way 'stupid girls' behave, and speaking as if she is a stupid girl herself.

Synopsis

Pink describes the ways in which stupid girls draw attention to themselves, hoping to attract a rich 'sugar daddy' to pay for their champagne lifestyle. They have abandoned any plans for a serious career in favour of going round to clubs in groups of two or three and behaving provocatively to get themselves noticed.
The singer then comments that she cannot take very much more of this irresponsible behaviour.
After a break she takes on the persona of a stupid girl and causes herself to vomit because she has just taken in more than 300 calories (the usual word for binge-eating followed by induced vomiting is *bulimia*), and desperately wants to be (fashionably) skinny. She is torn between wanting to act in a way which will attract a (rich) man, and not wanting to behave stupidly.

Unterrichtsempfehlungen

Die Vorbereitung der *pre-reading activity* kann von einer Schülerin/einem Schüler übernommen werden, indem sie/er für das Plenum Kurzinformationen zu Fred Segal und „50 Cent“ vorstellt. Der Kurs kann danach im Sinne der *pre-reading activity* seine Spekulationen äußern.

Fred Segal – clothing boutique owner
50 Cent – American rapper
(Information via Wikipedia)

We can safely assume that these people and the boutiques are part of the 'celeb' culture which the stupid girls would dearly love to become a part of but are doomed to fail.

Die Ergebnisse zu den Aufgaben 1. a) und b) sollten stichpunktartig an der Tafel festgehalten werden. Vor dieser Folie kann dann der 2. Aufgabenstellung folgend eine fundierte, textbezogene Diskussion stattfinden.
Die dritte Aufgabe beinhaltet sicherlich ein hohes Maß an Motivation. Die Lehrkraft kann die Aufgabe als Referat an einige interessierte Schülerinnen und Schüler vergeben. Eine andere Möglichkeit besteht darin, dass jeder Schüler in Form einer sehr kurzen Präsentation einen Song benennt, das Thema des gewählten Liedtextes skizziert und die Bezüge zum Liedtext von Pink benennt.

Solutions

Activities p. 54

1. **a) In pairs, work out how “Stupid Girls” are characterized and criticized in the song.**
   Points to make:
   – want to attract sexy/rich/well-known men/paparazzi – but know their provocative behaviour is stupid
   – flip back their blond hair/push up their bras
   – go to all the 'right' boutiques, clubs etc. to rub shoulders with celebrities/buy the right clothes and accessories
   – have abandoned all attempts to do anything 'serious' or ambitious with their lives
   – induce vomiting to remain thin/skinny
   – the basic criticism right through the song is that 'stupid girls' know what they are doing *is* stupid, but they are compulsively driven to behave in the way described in the hope of becoming or attracting some kind of 'celeb'

b) In groups, discuss the role of TV and the media as reflected in the song. Present your findings to the class.
Possible comment:
The girls in question know that this is the way to behave if you want to get yourself photographed by the paparazzi, become a minor celeb etc. because they have seen coverage of young women like themselves in magazines such as *Hello*, on TV and in films for their kind of audience. They know about women who are famous for being famous such as the so-called WAG's in England (Wives And Girlfriends of the national football team) and style themselves to look as similar to them as possible.

2. **Do you agree with Pink's view on girls dancing in videos etc.? Discuss your ideas in class.**
There will probably be mixed reactions here, ranging from the famous slogan 'girls just wanna have fun' to planning for the future/going to university etc., trying to look attractive and at the same time being taken seriously as a person, resisting anorexia/bulimia in spite of the emaciated models used by leading fashion houses.

3. **Do you know a song that deals with a similar topic? Present your song to your class. Explain your thoughts and feelings about it or make a personal comment.**
e.g. Bros – When will I be famous?; Cyndi Lauper – Girls just wanna have fun; Christina Aguilera – Beautiful; ...

Additional activity

Write a song or poem with the title 'Stupid Boys'.
Some ideas:
- wearing sports gear but not doing any actual sport
- spending most of their spare time playing violent computer games
- getting drunk/smoking to show how clever/adult they are
- showing off to impress the girls
- dressing in a special scruffy kind of way to demonstrate membership of the peer group
- not knowing how to talk to girls
- not taking enough care over personal hygiene

Coming Soon, the End of a Cinema Near You?

Ben Macintyre

Text

The text deals with the changing world of film. Whereas in the past there was only one way to watch a film – in a cinema – now there are all kinds of alternatives. However, the author believes that the 'classic' way to watch films is a special kind of experience which will survive.

Synopsis

Until quite recently everyone watched films in cinemas, but this is changing. Recently a large producer of adult entertainment (soft pornography) said that in future customers could burn DVDs of their films off the web. It is also possible to watch films on computers, iPods or mobile phones. This means that we can watch whatever we want at any time, and also take a break, skip boring bits, freeze frames and so on. We can even make our own films by remixing material from one or more films, although this is more or less illegal. Americans are now twice as likely to watch a DVD as a film in the cinema, and young people spend more time online than watching television. However, even when films are released simultaneously in the cinema, on DVD and on television, the writer believes that the cinema will survive. It provides a social, shared moment which intensifies the experience. Nothing else really compares.

Unterrichtsempfehlungen

Die Schülerinnen und Schüler fertigen vor der Lektüre des Textes im Rahmen der *pre-reading activity* in Einzelarbeit eine Liste mit Gründen für die Sorgen der Filmstudios (fear of piracy) an. Folgende Punkte könnten genannt werden:

- *less people will pay to see the film in the cinema*
- *the studios will lose money*
- *in the long run cinemas may have to close*
- *the studios will no longer be in control*
- *their intellectual copyright is being ignored/violated*

Die Auseinandersetzung mit dem Text bietet vielfaltige Sprechanlässe. Insbesondere die Aufgaben 1 und 3 laden zu kontroversen Unterrichtsgesprächen ein. Die Aufgaben 2 a) und 2 b) hingegen sollten schriftlich, in Form einer Hausaufgabe oder aber in einer Stillarbeitsphase, gelöst werden. Es bietet sich den Lernenden hier die Chance, ihre Schreibroutine zu festigen.

Solutions

Activities p. 56

1. **"Coming soon, the end of a cinema near you?" Comment on the headline. Why has the journalist put it as a question?**
   Points to make:
   - The words "coming soon ... to a cinema near you" are the classic formula for introducing a trailer or other form of advertisement for a new film.
   - With so much competition from other media, it certainly looks as if the cinema is under threat.
   - However, Macintyre formulates his title as a question because he thinks that reports of the death of the cinema have been much exaggerated.
   - He believes that cinema provides a unique experience.

2. **a) What effects is the digital revolution having on film and television?**
   - Cheap DVDs can be bought or burnt.
   - There is no need to go to the cinema.
   - Films can also be viewed on the Internet or on various small mobile devices (with tiny screens!).
   - Viewers can contribute their own videos for viewing on the web.
   - 'Official' films and TV have lost their 'stand alone' status and some of their authority.
   - However, as so much non-professional material is of dreadful quality and in doubtful taste, there may well be a backlash in favour of the traditional media from time to time.

   b) How are online viewers becoming a part of the creative process of making a film or television programme? Give reasons or find examples.
   Some points that could be made:
   - Generally speaking, the people who actually make films and TV programmes are doing this kind of work because they are very good at it – the competition is intense.
   - It would be very hard to integrate work from 'outsiders' into the planning and shooting of films or TV programmes.
   - There is of course already some consumer participation in TV programmes, but the format is under the control of the professionals.

– Nevertheless, it is quite possible that 'outsiders' could contribute via computer links to the production team of a TV programme or film.
– It is questionable whether these contributions would actually be welcomed, except in the case of programmes/films requiring specialist knowledge or skills not available in the core team.

3. **Do you agree that "there is nothing to compare with a packed cinema, an intimate friend and a bucket of fresh popcorn"? Why? Why not?**
Personal statements which will depend on whether the students enjoy the cinema atmosphere or not. Some ideas:
positive:
– The darkness makes the experience more intense.
– You share the emotions of the other cinema-goers, so they are intensified somehow – a mass audience experience.
– It's nice to go to the cinema with a boyfriend/girlfriend.
– It's an evening out instead of an evening stuck at home.
– You can get refreshments to eat/drink as you watch the film.
– Even wide screen TV can't compare with the really big screen and 'surround sound' in a cinema.
negative:
– Cinema tickets are expensive – home entertainment is generally cheap once you have got the equipment.
– It's nicer at home with all your own stuff around you.
– It's easier to watch at home than it is to get up and go out.
– A crowded cinema can be a bit claustrophobic.
– You can stop and start the film when you want, freeze frames, watch in slow motion or skip the boring bits.
– You don't have to sit through half an hour of commercials before the film starts.

Worksheet 5

Vocabulary – Talking about the Media

Expressions	Verdicts	
Did you see ... There was something really ... on I thought ... was ... ... was very good as the ... My favourite ... is ... Have you read ... I couldn't put it down It was a real page-turner Once put down, ... was hard to pick up again I can't stand ... I thought the plot was ... What was it about? What happened then/next/later/after that? I would have thought ... I didn't quite get the point (about ...) I didn't think (very) much of ...	interesting exciting/thrilling gripping boring frightening (not very) convincing (not very) realistic life-changing entertaining/amusing/funny (pure) fantasy well/badly-written/acted disjointed dramatic spine-chilling not my cup of tea might interest older/younger people	
Characters	**Parts**	**TV Programmes**
hero(ine) villain detective good/bad cops/guys minor character(s) (main) protagonist comic/stock characters two-dimensional characters convincing/three dimensional characters	plot background setting introduction exposition build-up climax (re)solution conclusion	news science documentary police drama soap opera comedy nature/quiz programme sports reality TV

Activities

1. **Use the material above to write a dialogue between two people, one of whom has seen or read a film/TV programme or book recently, and the other hasn't.**

2. **Write a review of a film/TV programme/book/newspaper article which you have seen or read recently.**
   Some hints:
   – Write a proper introduction answering the appropriate 'wh-questions' (see the worksheet for the chapter on newspapers).
   – Give some details of plot, characters etc., and express your opinion about them.
   – But don't give away the main point of the story etc.
   – Use comparisons with other similar material if they help to throw light on the film etc. in question (gives you the chance to show off your own knowledge!).
   – Conclude with a general verdict and a recommendation to view/read or not, as the case may be.

Worksheet 5 Solution

1. Guided dialogue and review based on the vocabulary provided. The dialogue could begin as follows:
   A: Did you see the film last night?
   B: I only watched the first few minutes. It was boring.
   A: Ah, you're saying that because you don't like action films.
   B: Well, they're just not realistic, are they.
   A: That's not the point. An action film is supposed to ...
   B: What happened after I went to bed?
   A: Well, ...

2. The review could begin along the following lines:
   I recently read a novel by Donna Leon.
   As usual the novel was set in Venice, and the main character was her popular detective, Commissario Brunetti. The story was gripping from the start. I enjoyed the way the beautiful, but sometimes sinister background of Venice was evoked.
   The good characters ...
   The villain(s) ...
   The plot ...
   Some people feel that Leon makes too much use of clichés, but this reader ...
   I can thoroughly recommend this book for readers who ...

Steam Radio – Still a 'Hot' Medium?

About the photograph

During the years before, during and after the Second World War, there is no doubt that radio was the prime medium in the home (the cinema was paramount outside the home as television was still in its infancy). The photograph is one of many which showed the nuclear or extended family gathered round the set, usually a large, wooden object – almost a piece of furniture. People were shown listening seriously or light-heartedly, depending on the kind of programme, or (as in this photograph) discussing what they were listening to.

What's on the Radio Today/Time to Tune in

Unterrichtsempfehlungen

Die Lektüre des einleitenden Textes in Verbindung mit der Schwarz-Weiß-Fotographie aus dem Jahr 1951 sollte gemeinsam im Plenum vorgenommen werden. Im Anschluss sollten die Schülerinnen und Schüler im Rahmen einer Spontanphase Gelegenheit haben, auf Text und Fotographie und die damit in Verbindung stehenden Impulse reagieren zu können. Danach sollte in einer Partnerarbeitsphase „What's on the Radio Today?" angegangen werden. Die Lehrkraft sollte betonen, dass es Ziel ist, am Ende der Partnerarbeitsphase einige Themenbereiche der verschiedenen Programme benennen und darüber hinaus einen kurzen Kommentar abgeben zu können („What kinds of material are you likely to find on the different programmes?"/„Make some general comments about the programmes in both senses.").
Die Anregungen unter „Time to Tune in" eröffnen vielfältige Herangehensweisen. Abhängig von der Ausstattung der Schule könnten beispielsweise die Aufgaben 1 – 4 in einem Computerraum der Schule in Kleingruppen (3 bis max. 4 Schüler, nicht mehr!) erarbeitet werden. Den Schülerinnen und Schülern müssen dabei Kopfhörer zur Verfügung stehen. Der Arbeitsprozess der Kleingruppen folgt der Strukturierung, die durch die Arbeitsanweisungen 1 – 4 gegeben ist und sollte in eine kleine Präsentation münden (vgl. dazu die Anregungen in Aufgabe 4), bei der der Einsatz eines Beamers denkbar ist. Alternativ könnten die Aufgaben 14 aber auch zu Hause in Einzelarbeit erledigt werden. Im Unterricht werden dann von der Lehrkraft mithilfe des Losverfahrens einige Schülerinnen und Schüler für Präsentationen ermittelt.

Solutions

Text and programme p. 57/58

See if you can make some general comments about the programmes, in both senses.

Radio 1
Popular music programmes introduced by DJs (disc jockeys), with a very small amount of news

Radio 2
Broadly similar, but with some features and radio plays/serials (Sexton Blake)

Radio 3
Nearly all classical music, including full-length concerts (the Proms – promenade concerts) with some serious features and news broadcasts

Radio 4
A very wide range of non-musical programmes, generally of high quality and appealing to well-educated listeners

Radio 5 Live
A mix of pop music, film reviews and sports reporting

Classic FM
Lighter classical music

World Service
Mainly news from all over the world; the BBC is proud of the fact that people in other countries listen to 'the BBC' (in this case the World Service) when they want to find out what is really happening in their own countries.

BBC Radio 7
A kaleidoscope of (mainly) old radio serials, including detective series, comedy and serious fiction (e.g. Agnes Grey, a novel by Anne Brontë)

Hallo

Stephen Fry

Text — This text is an almost complete transcription of a half-hour radio programme about the word 'Hallo'. The programme was the last part of a series of programmes about the English language presented and to a large degree written by Stephen Fry.

Synopsis — (See Activities 1 and 5 below)

Unterrichtsempfehlungen

Das recht umfangreiche Transkript sollte von den Schülerinnen und Schülern vorab im Rahmen einer Hausaufgabe gelesen werden. Stichpunktartig sollten die Lernenden dabei die in grün gedruckten Fragen am rechten Rand des Textes beantworten. Es empfiehlt sich darüber hinaus, die Schülerinnen und Schüler im Vorfeld auf die Vokabelangaben am Ende einer jeden Seite aufmerksam zu machen und sie dazu aufzufordern, sich mit diesen in ihrer für den Text relevanten Konnotation vertraut zu machen. Die Aufgabe 1 kann in einer Gruppenarbeitsphase gelöst werden. Der Kurs wird dabei den Oberbegriffen folgend in 6 Gruppen eingeteilt, wobei jede Gruppe von der Lehrkraft ein Plakat erhält. Die Plakate sollten dann in einem Galeriegang präsentiert werden und können im weiteren Verlauf der Unterrichtsreihe im Kursraum hängen bleiben. Deshalb ist eine ansprechende und gut lesbare Gestaltung der Plakate erforderlich.
Die Aufgabe 2 lädt zu szenischem Spiel ein und kann in Partnerarbeit angegangen werden. Anschließend ist es denkbar, einige Partner ihr „Hallo" präsentieren zu lassen, wobei das Plenum die Wirkung zu interpretieren und beurteilen hat. Erst danach sollten die Vorführenden ihre Einschätzungen mitteilen. Andere Partner können darauf reagieren, sich beteiligen und ihre Erkenntnisse ergänzend einbringen. Ein Unterrichtsgespräch, das dem Impuls von Aufgabe 3 folgt, rundet den Arbeitsprozess schlüssig ab. Die Aufgaben 4 und 5 sollten schriftlich erarbeitet werden – entweder in einer Phase der Stillarbeit oder als Hausaufgabe. Aufgabe 4 kann in Form von Stichpunkten gelöst werden, während Aufgabe 5 zu einem vollständigen Text führen sollte. Dabei können die Schülerinnen und Schüler das ihnen mit dem Text (neu) begegnete Vokabular berücksichtigen.

Solutions

While-reading tasks p. 59

There are two verbal jokes in the title of the series. Can you explain them?
Fry's – the name of the presenter and of a chocolate manufacturer who makes 'Fry's Turkish Delight'; 'English Delight' – word play on Turkish Delight

What role does 'hallo' play here?
This is the kind of 'hallo' which is used when someone is desperately trying to get a reply when calling the emergency services (via an operator in this case).

How has Fry used 'hallo' here?
He has used it to remind Butterfield that he is supposed to be giving a coherent, sensible reply to Fry's request for a definition instead of mumbling.

While-reading tasks p. 60

There's short break in the programme at this point. What is Fry's little game with the listener?
He points out that people who are only interested in 'Hallo' as a greeting don't need to know any more about the word, and can try another programme or do something else entirely at this point, hence the short break, which could be the end of the programme. Most people will, of course, want to know more – and they are greeted with 'Hallo? Good, you're still with us.'

What might the brown envelope contain?
In this kind of context, brown envelopes usually contain money from a doubtful source, or a bribe.

While-reading tasks p. 62

Can you explain this metaphor (a 'grey squirrel' of a usage')
Grey squirrels came across from North America, and are seen by many British people as unwelcome intruders, who have pushed out the native red squirrels in many parts of the country. In the same way, 'Hallo' as a greeting (also imported from America) has pushed out native forms of greeting such as 'What cheer?'

Where does this image (marking his territory) come from?
It refers to the way in which various animals (foxes, for example) use urine to mark their territory, i.e. tell other animals that they claim the area so marked.

What is the joke exactly?
As so often with jokes, it's a question of expectations fulfilled or not, as the case may be. Here we would normally expect the wife to be shocked and upset to be caught *in flagrante* but she is only upset not to be greeted with a fourth 'hello'. **Note**: Fry spells hallo with an 'a' in the title of the programme, but 'hello' seems better in the joke above. 'Hullo' is also possible – there are no important differences between the three spellings.

Activities p. 63

1. **The broadcast has been divided into sections for you to make it more manageable. Sum up what is said about 'hallo' in a few brief notes for each section:**

   Aircrew
   - straightforward greeting
   - if another greeting is used, this could be a coded message to another stewardess

   Butterfield (1)
   - meaning depends on the context/the function

   Butterfield (2)
   - standard greeting
   - asking if someone is still there
   - expressing surprise
   - reminding someone to start behaving properly/politely

Clayton

- 'Hallo' has evolved from a hunting cry

Hope

- Shakespeare does not use 'Holla' as a greeting in the modern sense
- link with hunting still strong
- greetings in Shakespeare include 'how now', 'how doth', what cheer?' etc.
- The last of these greetings in particular would expect an answer.
- 'Wotcher' is a form of 'what cheer' which survived in music hall songs into the twentieth century (and was still in use in Wiltshire when the editor was a boy).

Koenigsberg

- first recorded in North America 1827
- used there in a newspaper as a call to attention and a greeting combined
- used as a greeting in a book by Davy Crockett in 1833
- Dickens used 'Hallo' as a greeting in A *Christmas Carol* in 1843.
- In the same story it is also used as a shout or exclamation.
- Koenigsberg suggests that Dickens may have picked up 'Hallo' as a greeting while he was in America in 1842.
- He also points out that Edison suggested 'hallo' as the best word to use instead of a bell when telephoning (early telephones must have functioned differently!).

2. **Using information from the text, try out some different ways of saying 'Hallo' on a partner. How does he or she interpret them? Do you agree with one another? Report your results to the class.**
   (Free activity – various ways of saying 'hallo' are covered in the text.)

3. **How is 'Hallo' used in German? Have there been any changes over the past few years? What German words of greeting do you know? Don't forget the regional variations.**
   Points which could be made:
   - used to tell someone they have said or done something unacceptable: *Aber Hallo*!
   - used to attract attention
   - used as a greeting
   - The use as a greeting has definitely become more widespread over the last few years, often replacing *Guten Tag* etc. in shops, for example.
   - regional variations, e. g.:
     – moin (North Germany)
     – Tag! (very widespread)
     – Grüß Gott (South Germany)
     – Servus (South Germany, Austria)

4. **Unfortunately you can't listen to this programme live any more. Think of some additional kinds of information which a listener would have access to.**
   Points which could be made:
   - social class of the speaker
   - level of education of the speaker
   - regional accents
   - use of emphatic intonation to make a point
   - use of irony
   - attitude of the speaker to what he/she is saying (favourable or unfavourable, etc.)
   - interaction/reactions as speakers respond to one another
   - mood (angry, happy, etc.)
   - age of the speaker in some cases

5. Write a brief history of the word 'hallo' based on Stephen Fry's radio programme. Include a sentence or two on other greetings that have failed to survive up to the present day.

Sample answer:
It is generally agreed that the word 'Hallo' was first used as part of a call or cry used by hunters during the period after the Norman Conquest. In Shakespeare's day the word was still generally used as an exclamation, or to attract attention. Other expressions are used as greetings in Shakespeare, such as 'How now?', 'Well met' and 'What cheer?'. This last greeting survived into modern times via the music hall, where it evolved into 'Wotcher'. The use of 'hallo' as a greeting is recorded first in North America in the 1820s and 1830s. When Dickens uses the word in this way in *A Christmas Carol*, he may have heard 'hallo' used as a greeting during his visit to America in 1842. Edison thought 'hallo' would be the right word to use when telephoning.

Yesterday's Tomorrows – Future Imperfect?

Illustration The illustration is an example of the kind of picture which used to appear in early publications, comics etc. which dealt with the future. Inevitably the artists got some aspects of the future 'right' and others 'wrong'.

Solutions

Illustration p. 64 **Which features of the drawing above have 'come true', and which haven't?**

have come true

- e.g. skyscrapers, rockets urban rail systems, deep sea adventures (diving is popular, but really deep sea exploration is reserved for scientists)

have not come true

- flying cars (of early postwar design – an interesting clash of out of date and modern ideas)
- airships (except in very limited applications, e.g. used for advertising)
- trips to the moon (but it is possible to book a stay at the ISS International Space Station if you are a millionaire)

Computers ... don't feature at all. Why might that be?

The likely answer is that it was impossible for authors to imagine even a few of the things which computers have turned out to be capable of. Neither calculating machines nor (electric) typewriters (the closest 'ancestors') gave the slightest hint of the future potential of computers. Who imagined that most people would use computers to deal with their mail, their photographs, keep in touch with friends, do a good deal of their shopping, perhaps find a partner, play very complex and realistic games, ... when they saw the first clumsy machines, which were in fact like huge calculators or electric typewriters? And we ourselves don't know what will come next.

The editor saw a very early computer called LEO when he was looking for a job in the 1960s. It consisted of a long, narrow office entirely filled with huge grey boxes – and it was less powerful than a basic laptop today.

Additional activity **Although computers do not appear in major SF works, some authors were already thinking a long way ahead. What features of working with modern computers can you find in the following extract:**

In 1946, an astonishingly complete vision of the future appeared in the magazine Astounding Science Fiction. In a story entitled "A Logic Named Joe", the author Murray Leinster envisioned a world in which every home was equipped with a tabletop box that he called a "logic".

"You got a logic in your house. It looks like a vision receiver used to, only it's got keys instead of dials and you punch the keys for what you wanna get ... you punch 'Sally Hancock's Phone' an' the screen blinks an' sputters an' you're hooked up with the logic in her house an' if somebody answers you got a visionphone connection. But besides that, if you punch for the weather forecast for who was mistress of the White House durin' Garfield's administration ... that comes on the screen too. The relays in the tank do it. The tank is a big buildin' full of all the facts in creation ... hooked in with all the other tanks all over the country ... The only thing it won't do is tell you exactly what your wife meant when she said, 'Oh, you think so, do you?' in that peculiar kinda voice."

Oliver Burkeman, "Forty years of the internet: how the world changed forever", from *The Guardian*, 23.10.09

Solution to additional activity

Possible answers:
e. g. Keypad, Internet telephoning, Skype, Google, Wikipedia

The Veldt

Ray Bradbury

Author

Ray Douglas Bradbury (born August 22, 1920) is an American literary, fantasy, horror, science fiction, and mystery writer best known for *The Martian Chronicles*, a 1950 book which has been described both as a short story collection and a novel, and his 1953 dystopian novel *Fahrenheit 451*.
Fahrenheit 451 is a frightening dystopian vision of a world in which books are burned because they are considered subversive (likely to threaten the government). The fire service burns books (and houses with books in them) rather than putting out fires. People who don't conform are pursued and killed by a 'Mechanical Hound'. The hero, Montag, is a fireman who starts to question what is going on, and ends up on the run from the Hound.

Synopsis

(See Activity 1 below)

Unterrichtsempfehlungen

Die Lektüre der umfangreichen Kurzgeschichte „The Veldt" sollte von den Schülerinnen und Schülern vorab geleistet werden. Die Schülerinnen und Schüler sollten von der Lehrkraft auf die *Annotations* am unteren Rand der Seiten aufmerksam gemacht werden und die Aufgabe erhalten, im Rahmen der Lektüre die in grün gedruckten Fragen am rechten Rand der Seiten stichpunktartig zu beantworten. Jede Schülerin/jeder Schüler sollte darüber hinaus bis zu fünf Nomen oder Verben aus der Geschichte heraussuchen und diese auf eine Karte schreiben. Es sollten Wörter sein, die wesentliche Handlungszusammenhänge der Geschichte spiegeln. In einer Unterrichtsstunde sollte sich die Lehrkraft der Sicherung des Textverständnisses widmen. Dazu können die auf Karten geschriebenen Wörter verwendet werden. Zunächst in Gruppen, dann im Plenum, müssen per Losverfahren Schülerinnen und Schüler ebenfalls nach dem Zufallsprinzip ausgewählte Wortkarten vor dem Hintergrund ihres Textverständnisses erklären.
Nach der Sicherung des Textverständnisses kann der Aufgabenapparat angegangen werden, dessen Aufgaben 1 – 4 in schriftlicher Form erledigt werden sollten, da sie sich als hervorragende Vorbereitung auf schriftliche Abitur- bzw. Klausuraufgaben eignen. Da es sich um eine Übung handelt, ist es durchaus denkbar, dass die Schülerinnen und Schüler die Aufgaben gemeinsam in Teams verschriftlichen – entweder im Rahmen von 3 Unterrichtsstunden oder aber als Hausaufgabe, bei der die Teams sich durch E-Mail austauschen. Abhängig von der aktuellen Belastung der Lehrkraft, sollte den Schülerinnen und Schülern die Möglichkeit eingeräumt werden, ihre Texte einreichen zu können.
Die Aufgabe 5 sollte in Partnerarbeit vorbereitet werden und anschließend zu einem Austausch im Plenum führen. Aufgabe 6 sollte hingegen als Hausaufgabe schriftlich erledigt werden, abhängig vom Vorwissen der Lerngruppe sollte die Lehrkraft wesentliche Merkmale eines Essays wiederholen oder aber den Schülerinnen und Schülern an die Hand geben.

Solutions

Before you read p. 65

What might [Bradbury] have got right – and wrong – when he thought and wrote about these issues in the 1950s?

Points which students could make:

- People in towns suffer from very high levels of noise pollution, especially those who live near main roads and airports.
- Plenty of teenagers and some adults become very unhappy if they cannot listen to their music at high volume during waking hours – or pump it directly into their ears.
- We already have virtual reality (see p. 47/48 of the students' book), but Bradbury's vision of whole virtual (or not so virtual!) landscapes goes much further than anything we can produce at present.
- It would be interesting to ask students whether they think computers will ever be able to produce (and/or transport) real objects, apart from photographs and printed paper.

While-reading task p. 65

Find some features in these lines which show we are in a 'futuristic' house.

E.g. the stove hums to itself, the house is soundproofed, the house clothes its owners, feeds them, and rocks them to sleep. Lights come on as they approach rooms and turn themselves off as they move on.

While-reading task p. 69

Explain the significance of the expression 'in a rut' as it is used here.

It means that the children have created the African scenario so many times that the equipment which produces it for them is now stuck and cannot be changed to other imagined scenes – like a cart on an old mud road with deep ruts which trap its wheels. (Ruts in modern motorways are dangerous for a different reason – the risk of aquaplaning.)

While-reading task p. 70

What could George's old wallet be doing in the nursery?

Bradbury never explains the significance of this incident, or the appearance of Lydia's bloodstained scarf (lines 393 – 599), so we can only speculate.

It seems likely that Bradbury imagined that the children gave these objects to the lions so that they could get the scent of the parents, and would therefore be more likely to attack them when the time was ripe.

While-reading task p. 71

Compare this exchange with what happens in more traditional father and son roles.

In this scene it is clear that all the real power is with the son, who uses a cold tone of voice to underline the fact that he means what he says, he disagrees with his father at every point (this occurs in more traditional father-son exchanges too, of course!) and makes real threats which it is clear the father has to take seriously: "I don't think you'd better consider it any more, Father."

While-reading task p. 72

'really nothing' – Do you agree with the psychologist?

'Violence, paranoia' – apparently these are normal among children in the world which Bradbury is describing, so we can assume that the psychologist comes across them all the time and is not bothered by serious behavioural disorders of this kind. We would not agree that the scientist is right to trivialise them but of course they do exist in our world too.

While-reading task p. 73

Santa Claus ... Scrooge: How does the psychologist use these characters to explain the children's changed feelings towards their parents?

In the past the parents were very indulgent towards their children, spoiled them in fact, as the psychologist says (line 353). So in a way every day was more or less like Christmas, with Santa Claus presiding. Now the parents want to switch off all the electronic equipment, including the nursery, so they are now treating the children as a miser would. They could afford to leave everything switched on, but they don't want to, just as a miser has money but doesn't want to spend it.

Comment on the sentence, 'Don't let father kill everything', paying special attention to the word 'kill'.
While-reading task p. 74

The use of the word 'kill' for inanimate objects suggests that the children no longer make a distinction between living beings and machines. It also implies that they will not see much difference between 'killing' a machine and killing people.

Can you explain the other screams?
While-reading task p. 75

(See also the comment on the wallet, while-reading task p. 70.) Again, Bradbury does not explain, but we can assume that somehow or other the lions are attacking and eating real prey, either other animals or people. The children will have played a role in supplying the lions with prey, but there is no hint in the story about missing pets or persons.

The last line seems like a bit of an anti-climax – or does it? Why do you think the author chose to end the story in this way?

Points which could be made;

- The author could have wanted to end on a peaceful, everyday note after violence which had gone before.
- He could want to show how callous the children have become – their parents have just been killed, but they have no problem behaving quite normally in a social situation – there is no sign of shock or remorse.
- Wendy probably wants to distract Mr. McClean's attention from the feeding lions in the distance. He might want to ask some awkward questions.

Activities p. 76

1. **Write an outline of the story in about half a dozen sentences.**
   The action takes place at some time in the future. George and Linda Hadley, who live in a very high-tech house, are worried about the way their children have become obsessed by an African scenario, which they can create in their nursery by using their imagination. There are lions in this African landscape which appear to be eating real prey of some kind. It becomes increasingly difficult to change from this landscape to something less threatening. Eventually the parents consult a psychologist, and decide to switch off the nursery, and the rest of their hi-tech equipment. This infuriates the children, who lock their parents in the nursery, where they are eaten by the lions.
2. **You probably know that short stories often have a 'surprise ending'. Is that the case here?**
   Possible answers:
   Yes – because the reader does not expect there to be real bloodshed in a virtual world/does not expect anything quite so drastic to happen to the parents.
   No – because we have learnt that the children can be extremely callous/have no respect for their parents/have become addicted to the African scene. The wallet and scarf which the lions have obviously had contact with can be seen as clues to what is going to happen as in a detective story.
3. **Read the descriptions of the veldt again, looking out for emotional or poetic language including similes and metaphors. Make a list of expressions which you find particularly effective, and try to explain how they 'work' on the reader.**
   - e.g. hot yellow sun – tropical climate evoked/created in the nursery
   - cool green smell of the hidden water hole – contrast/hint of welcome relief from the heat

- great rusty smell of animals – bringing in another sense to make the atmosphere more realistic
- smell of dust like a red paprika – simile to help the reader imagine the smell
- papery rustling of vultures – sinister, threatening sound, we know what vultures eat
- dusty upholstery smell – metaphor to reinforce the sense of smell
- like the yellow of an exquisite French tapestry – simile to convey the exact colour of the lions' eyes
- panting, dripping mouths – emotive language – we know the drips will be blood (similar uses of language whenever the nursery is being described)

4. Choose one of the following issues, and write a paragraph about it:

a) 'spoiled' children and adults

Points which could be made:

- People in industrial nations live in great comfort compared with the not so distant past.
- It is normal for adults to have labour-saving devices in their homes, good holidays, cars, stereo equipment, TVs, computers, etc.
- People who cannot afford these things feel that they are missing out on the good life, and would probably describe better-off people as spoiled.
- However, most of these things are now 'normal' in prosperous countries – it doesn't count as spoiled for families to have a dishwasher, for example.
- At some point, when children or adults have 'absolutely everything' and the children are clearly treated very indulgently, those who only have the 'normal' goodies, will say they are spoiled and feel resentful/jealous.

b) virtual reality

Points which could be made:

- See pages 47/48 of the Students' Book
- Excitement of very realistic video games
- Dangers of addiction
- Virtual worlds more exciting than the real one
- Danger of lack of contact with real people/the real world
- Violent virtual worlds/computer games may lead to violence in the real world (a disputed point among the experts), because feelings can become blunted/the line between virtual and real violence can become blurred/some people may feel an urge to 'try out' violent crimes which they have experienced electronically.

c) Including impossible elements

Points which could be made:

- Some science fiction stories keep to the laws of science – but there is no 'rule' which says they have to do so.
- Bradbury is making important points about the dangers of too much virtual reality, and he has the right, of course, to get his message across as dramatically as possible.
- 'Suspension of disbelief' is an important concept here. If the reader can believe (while reading the story) that the scene/the lions, etc. are real, then the writer has succeeded. If not, he hasn't. Quite a lot depends of the extent to which individual readers are prepared to go along with the story.

d) labour-saving devices in the home

Points which could be made:

- Interesting to try and decide at what point a device becomes a luxury – and which devices would come into this category (in Germany – or in the Amazon rain forest, for example).

- Is it actually good for people to perform household tasks themselves (rich people have never thought so)?
- Some people actually enjoy cleaning windows, scrubbing floors, etc. Why could this be? Does it apply to you – or any of your friends?
- Old saying: 'Cleanliness is next to godliness' – is it true? Does it matter how the cleanliness is achieved?

5. **What aspects of life in the future was Bradbury particularly worried about? Would he have seen trends in this direction when he wrote the story in 1951? Have things moved further in the 'wrong' direction in the meantime? List some relevant aspects of modern life and try to decide, one by one, how far Bradbury was right to warn us about them.**
   Points which could be made:
   - Bradbury's main worries: people could become spoiled/lazy if their houses were full of labour-saving devices.
   - At the time, very few people, in Europe at least, even had refrigerators, but vacuum cleaners and, to a lesser extent, washing machines were already around. So the trends at the time could hardly have seemed very threatening.
   - Virtual reality existed only within the pages of science fiction, and modern computers had not even been imagined. Bradbury thought virtual reality could get out of control and actually present a physical risk to users.
   - Bradbury would certainly think we have moved further in the 'wrong' direction in the meantime. We, or some of us, try to compensate for sedentary/lazy lives by taking part in sporting activities of one kind or another. Relevant aspects of modern life have been covered above, e.g. violent video games, virtual reality, too many labour-saving devices (no one even wants to get up to press buttons on the TV).
6. **'Science fiction is just light entertainment. You can't take it seriously.' How far do you agree? Write a short essay using this story and other science fiction material you have read or seen for your examples.**
   Personal writing. Students could be reminded that some science fiction is just conventional adventure fiction moved into the future, while other kinds of science fiction, particularly dystopian stories, are often intended as serious warnings about dangerous trends which the writer has perceived in life in his own day. Students should be reminded that it is important to include examples from their own reading/viewing.

Additional Activity

Write a short science fiction story. Here are some ideas, in case you can't think of anything:
- The parents in "The Veldt" escape, and decide to punish their children appropriately.
- People become so lazy as a result of their comfortable lives that they never leave their houses any more – until there is some kind of threat which they will have to react to. (See *A Very Private Life* by Michael Frayn and "The Machine Stops" by E. M. Forster)
- Tiny, very cultured little creatures from another planet land on our earth. What happens to them? How could we communicate with them? (See "Meteor" by John Wyndham)
- Our planet is gradually becoming uninhabitable. What could we do about it? Some people are prepared to head off into space to look for another earth-like planet. Who would be chosen? How would the rest of the population react?
- Your dystopia. What would be the worst possible world you could personally imagine? Would you take on the classic role of the rebel? Could you succeed in changing things for the better?

The Murderer

Ray Bradbury

Synopsis

A man called Albert Brock has been arrested because he has been wrecking sound equipment of various kinds at home, at the office, in his car, and in the bus on his way home. As the story begins, he is being interviewed by a psychiatrist. Before the interview he has 'killed' the radio in the interview room, and he then destroys the psychiatrist's wrist radio. He explains that he feels oppressed on all sides by senseless sounds, different kinds of music which clash, people calling on the telephone, his boss supervising him via his car radio, and through the intercommunication system at work. He destroys all this equipment in various ways, and inevitably gets himself into trouble with the police. He is unrepentant, and hopes other people will begin to see things his way as his campaign has had worldwide media coverage. The psychiatrist is quite happy with things the way they are.

Unterrichtsempfehlungen

Von den Schülerinnen und Schülern sollte eine Vorab-Lektüre der umfangreichen Bradbury short story geleistet werden. Die Unterrichtsarbeit muss sich dann zunächst auf die Sicherung des Textverständnisses richten. In Kleingruppen könnten die Lernenden beispielsweise den Auftrag erhalten, den Inhalt der Geschichte zu besprechen und sich dann auf ein Zitat aus der Geschichte zu einigen, welches ihrer Meinung nach sehr zentrale Aussagen der Geschichte spiegelt. Das Zitat kann auf eine OHP-Folie geschrieben werden, um es später dem Rest des Kurses zu präsentieren, der dann die Aufgabe erhält, vor dem Hintergrund des gewonnenen Textverständnisses auf das Zitat zu reagieren. Aufgabe 1 sollte ebenfalls in Kleingruppen angegangen werden. Die Schülerinnen und Schüler sollten Informationen aus der Geschichte zu den Unterpunkten a), b) und c) sammeln und gut lesbar auf Karten/DIN-A4-Blätter schreiben. Die Lehrkraft kann während der Partnerarbeitsphase eine groß angelegte Tabelle auf die aufgeklappte Tafel schreiben. Anschließend können dann nach dem Losverfahren ausgwählte Kleingruppen ihre Ergebnisse an der Tafel einordnen und anheften. Das Plenum sollte dann im Anschluss – falls erforderlich – Aspekte ergänzen oder die Ergebnisse kommentieren und auf ihre Stichhaltigkeit hin überprüfen. Die folgenden Aufgaben des Aufgabenapparates bieten zum einen intensive Schreibanlässe und zum anderen ergiebige Sprechanlässe. Insbesondere die Aufgaben 2 – 4 und die Aufgabe 9 könnten Gespräche bzw. eine Diskussion im Plenum in Gang bringen. Es empfiehlt sich jedoch grundsätzlich, den Schülerinnen und Schülern vor einem Plenumsgespräch Zeit für eine Orientierung im Sinne der Aufgabenstellungen zu geben.

Solutions

Before you read p. 76

Other kinds of assaults on our senses ...

e.g. smell: diesel fumes, tobacco smoke, solvents as used in paint etc.

taste: anything you personally don't like eating or drinking, artificial flavours, too much salt, etc.

touch: coarse materials, some people can't touch certain materials without shuddering, e.g. velvet

vision: very bright/fluorescent colours, bad architecture, clashes of various kinds, e.g. tall block dwarfing church next to it

Why does the writer include such a mixture of different kinds of music?
While-reading tasks p. 77

He wants to show that there is no coordination from one source of music to another, and that the result becomes completely meaningless (and would give many people a headache unless this is what they like and are used to).

Comment on the fact that the prisoner smiles at the psychiatrist, although he says 'Go away'.

Various answers are possible, e. g.

- the 'murderer' (Albert Brock) is mad
- he is so pleased to have achieved silence in the interview room that he feels like smiling – but he still wants the psychiatrist to go away
- he doesn't care what happens to him any more – has lost his normal sense of responsibility

What do the emotive expressions in this line tell you about Brock's state of mind?
While-reading tasks p. 79

That he had arrived at a major turning point in his life, which could have very serious consequences

'Pawed ... mauled ... massaged ... pounded' – Explain the effect which these words have on the reader when they are used to describe sound.

They make sound seem as if it has a powerful physical effect on the listener. He will feel as if he has been involved in a fight – or a tough physiotherapy session.

Explain and comment on the imagery used to describe the televisor/television in these lines.
While-reading tasks p. 81

The Medusa image suggests that people who watch a lot of television sit still and stop thinking, almost as if they have been turned to stone. The Siren image underlines the addictive quality which television has for some people, and also suggests that the rewards for watching are minimal. If we pursue the Siren image further, it implies that too much television can lead to a mental breakdown.

What do you make of the psychiatrist's diagnosis?
While-reading tasks p. 82

He thinks that Brock is quite happy, but in a state of complete opposition to his environment. He is not seen as a serious danger to society (presumably he will be kept in prison, so he can't do any more damage). In the psychiatrist's terms Brock is mad, in our terms he would probably seem a bit strange to most people (the smiling, the sheer destructiveness), but we would probably feel some sympathy with his views and actions. The psychiatrist is not 'normal' in our terms either.

1. **Draw a wide, three-column table, and head the columns as follows, then go through the story and find the information you need to fill in the table.**
Activities p. 83

a) Brock's pet hates	b) Reasons for hating them	c) MO for 'killing' them
radio (here) in the interview room	prefers silence	kicked the radio to death
wrist radio	no escape from two-way communication, commercials, etc.	cracked it like a walnut
telephone	we can assume that he hates the telephone ringing, it seems impersonal, drains away personality, no warmth, easy to say the wrong thing, easy to make enemies, too convenient, makes you want to call someone – and makes other people want to call you whether there is any reason for the call or not, no time left for himself	put it in the insinkerator
television	(see pre-reading task, p. 81)	shot the cathode ray tube

radio, record player, cinema, films and commercials projected onto clouds, music by Mozzak in every restaurant, commercials on busses ...	very general dislike of everything which interferes with peace and quiet	
interoffice communication system	we can assume that he never feels free from supervision, interference with his work	poured water into the system
car radio	constant surveillance, pressure not to waste the firm's time, required to log off every time he leaves the car	spooned chocolate ice-cream into the radio
other people's wrist radios and the bus entertainment system	hearing other people's conversations, plus music and commercials from the bus's loudspeakers is an unbearable cacophony for him	hires a diathermy machine which blocks all the radio signals (and causes panic on the bus)
his house	The house talks, sings, hums, reports the weather, plays music at all hours, screams opera in the shower, teaches Spanish in your sleep and also has a speaking cooker/stove a front door which reminds you to wipe you feet, plus a vacuum hound which snuffles round behind you picking up debris. Feels that the house barely tolerates humans.	Intends to 'murder' it, starts by shooting the talking front door, the stove and the television, and putting the telephone in the Insinkerator (which was actually 'innocent' in his view). Then the police come for him.

2. **It's not just sounds which worry Brock. He dislikes the content, too. Why, exactly? There are several different reasons, depending on the source of noise (and vision). Find and comment on his objections to what the various media are saying to him (in some cases we are left to draw our own conclusions.**
   - music in the office – an unholy, senseless mixture, no one can appreciate any single kind of music
   - radio in the interview room – unnecessary background noise, disturbing thoughts
   - wrist radio – senseless non-stop communication, including public opinion polls which he hates
   - telephone – see above
   - music by Mozzek – (as for the radio in the interview room)
   - office intercommunication system – (see above)
   - car radio – can't escape from his boss/supervisor
   - on the bus – a combination of other people's pointless wrist radio conversations and a mix of music and commercials from the bus entertainment system.
   - house – 'barely tolerates humans'; feels as if he is constantly being told off and given instructions
   - television – (see Before you read p. 82)

3. **Why do you think he sees himself as a 'murderer', when he only attacks machines?**
   In his perhaps slightly disturbed mind, all these machines have begun to acquire personality/are personally attacking him/are almost human in some ways, so stopping them is more or less like killing real people.

4. **Are there any signs that his campaign could succeed?**
   His campaign has been covered on television, so a lot of people know about it. He says 'any day now', for signs that there could be a change in people's attitudes, but he is probably going to be disappointed, as everyone else seems happy in this environment. To some extent they are brainwashed/conditioned by it, so they feel deprived/ill at ease if the machines are turned off.

5. **There are several points in the story where the use of figurative language becomes quite dense. Find some of these areas, analyse the images, and try to explain what the author wanted to achieve by writing in this way.**
e. g. (line 65) "... some cold fish of a voice, all steel, copper, plastic, no warmth."
Here the author is emphasising the impersonal, disembodied quality of telephone communication (in the pre-Skype era, of course).
(line 96) "The Fourth of July on wheels!"
This is the big American celebration for the anniversary of the Declaration of Independence, with parties, flags flying, fireworks etc. There is the same kind of atmosphere in the office, except that in this case it is accompanied by panic (as if the office workers, who are 'addicted' to the intercommunication system, have suddenly had their 'drug' taken away from them).
(line 133) "It's a big bolt of the nicest, softest flannel ever made."
The author is trying to communicate the wonderful feeling of silence which Brock experiences when he has stopped the car radio. If we imagine holding a thick roll of flannel cloth to our ears, we can see what he means.
(line 147) "The 'Vienna Woods' chopped down, the canary mangled."
(lines 152 – 153) "Pandemonium, riot, and chaos. Squirrels chattering in cages."
These terms are used to show how violent cutting off familiar sounds is for those addicted to them (chopped, mangled), and how violent the withdrawal symptoms are for the people affected (pandemonium ... squirrels chattering in cages).
(line 191) "Oh how it sizzled and screamed, 'I'm shorted'."
The cooker/stove almost sounds as if it is human here – refers to itself in the first person singular (AE mainly stove, BE mainly cooker – but both terms are used in both countries).

6. **Comment on the repetition in the last few lines.**
These lines show that the psychiatrist is addicted, too. He needs to have his 'fix' of sounds repeated in a continuous cycle, and feels soothed, happy, as a result. Presumably he can only work efficiently when his sound levels are 'topped up' all the time in this way, like a drug.

7. **Write a paragraph in which you pick out and compare aspects of life in Brock's time and life today. Conclude with a personal comment on the role played by noise of all kinds in modern life.**
Points which could be made:
   - wrist radio – Used in just the same way as modern mobile phones, with the same effects.
   - telephone – We are at least as addicted to the telphone as people are in Brock's day. But we can add vision to sound via our computers – this could be seen as less impersonal. We have also added options such as video-conferencing.
   - Office inter-communication – Then and now supervisors can keep a very close watch on workers, can limit workers' access to confidential material – or put confidential material on the web/in the public domain. On the whole, we can do more, both good and bad, than Bradbury imagined.
   - television – Although some people leave the television on all the time, people are probably less interested in it/addicted than they were in the early days. Shows of various kinds are losing their almost universal appeal. Only major football matches/sports events generally attract the kind of audience which was quite common in the past, when everybody had watched – and wanted to talk about – the same programme(s) next morning at work.
   - background music in restaurants – Personal reactions vary widely according to personal taste, volume, mood, etc.

- commercials – Some people find them entertaining, others are infuriated by the advertisements themselves, the use of clichés, the endless repetition.
- car radio – Most people regard a car radio (+ CD player/MP3 player) as essential for entertainment, general news, weather and traffic news. These last features, which we can accept as genuinely useful/a contribution to road safety, do not play a role in Bradbury's view of the car radio.
- Brock's house – Some features of this house exist in ours. The richer people are, the more 'gimmicks' of this kind they are likely to have installed. We have not really reached the point where we feel that we are intruders in our own houses. However, parents quite often feel severely under attack from loud noise from teenagers' bedrooms.
- noise in modern life – Steadily increasing in urban areas, many people suffer – information about the noise produced by vacuum cleaners, lawnmower, leaf blowers ... plays a minor role in sales literature, etc. Airports, motorways, road-works are particularly severe sources of noise, along with the very loud music which seems to be essential at most festivals, fairs, etc.

8. **Are other 'threats' to the good life just as important, or more important than noise? Make a list of your own 'pet hates' and talk about them with your fellow-students.**
Likely issues:
the environment, politicians, quality of TV, lack of money, conditions in developing countries, wars, religious and ethnic differences/problems, intolerance generally, personal characteristics such as arrogance, lack of humour, status-seeking, certain makes of car/types of driver ...

9. **Think of some features of modern life which have become more or less normal, but which are questionable for other reasons. Talk about your ideas with your fellow-students. Perhaps everyone is 'out of step' on some issues.**
Free discussion. Some issues and useful expressions:
   - flying – marvellous! – the only way to get to nice holiday destinations – very bad for the environment should be banned – you must be joking!
   - mobile phones – great invention – can't live without it – couldn't keep in touch with friends without it – more and more other important stuff becoming available via the mobile phone – safety issue for children – why do people have to talk so loudly on their mobiles? – do they think we are all interested in what they are saying? – so much mobile phone talk is unnecessary, at least an SMS is silent and cheap.
   - driving children even small distances to school – 'the school run' – makes them lazy – bad for their health – danger of kidnapping, child abuse etc. – the world was a safer place a generation ago – was it really, or do the media blow up every little incident out of proportion?
   - teenagers spending a lot of time with their computers – my computer is my life, more or less – can do homework, play games, consult reference websites, find the best price/best range of goods for things to buy – order goods without having to go to the shops – makes work more efficient – can be used to cheat – can become addictive – problem of violent games – problem that children and teenagers spend less time out in the fresh air than they used to – couch potatoes, overweight, unfit.
   - Agreeing – disagreeing:
      - I can see what you mean, but ...
      - Anyone who (does that) must be crazy/out of their minds, I try not to spend too much time (doing ...) but I'm afraid ...
      - I don't know why you feel like that about ...
      - That's no problem as far as I'm concerned.

- I wouldn't dream of doing ...
- How would you cope with/manage/do ... if you couldn't/didn't have ...
- I wouldn't (do) ... myself, but I can understand/appreciate why some people ...
- I find ... really irritating/annoying.
- I have a bad conscience about ... but I'm afraid ...

Worksheet 6

I wouldn't say I'm addicted, but I do spend a lot of time ...

A Puzzle Page – Part I

The first puzzle is quite easy – just fill in the clues and find the key literary term which runs vertically down the grid

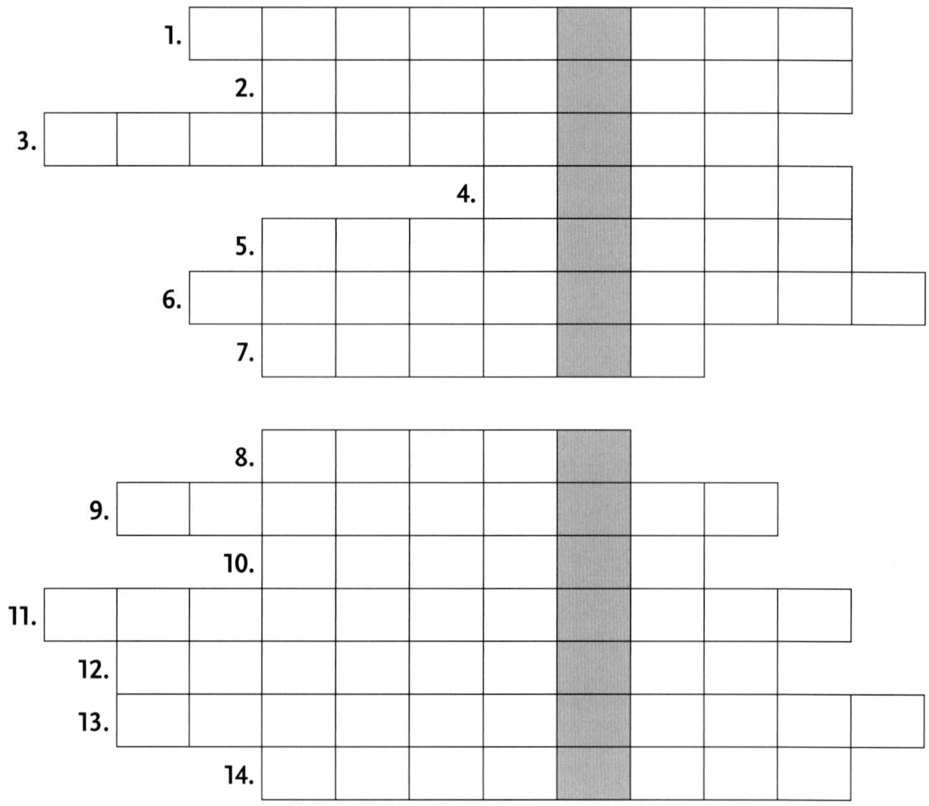

CLUES

1. Really wrapped up in what you are doing – like the children in their nursery
2. Right now
3. A nice flavour – the children's cheeks were this colour
4. The title of one of the stories: 'The ...'
5. State of mind when you think everyone is against you
6. If you are being ..., people are making your life a misery – or putting you in prison.
7. To interfere with something
8. One of these was bloodstained in the first story.
9. Pushing someone away – or rejecting their ideas
10. To hop or bounce around rather like a spirited horse
11. Device which sends out sound or vision signals
12. The study of the meanings of words
13. Noisy, chaotic state of affairs
14. Singing slowly and sentimentally

Worksheet 6 Solution

1.			E	N	G	R	O	**S**	S	E	D	
2.				D	I	R	E	**C**	T	L	Y	
3.	P	E	P	P	E	R	M	**I**	N	T		
4.							V	**E**	L	D	T	
5.				P	A	R	A	**N**	O	I	A	
6.			P	E	R	S	E	**C**	U	T	E	D
7.				T	A	M	P	**E**	R			

8.				S	C	A	R	**F**				
9.		R	E	P	U	L	S	**I**	N	G		
10.				P	R	A	N	**C**	E			
11.	T	R	A	N	S	M	I	**T**	T	E	R	
12.		S	E	M	A	N	T	**I**	C	S		
13.		P	A	N	D	E	M	**O**	N	I	U	M
14.				C	R	O	O	**N**	I	N	G	

Worksheet 7

A Puzzle Page – Part II

The second puzzle is a bit harder. It's not exactly cryptic like the puzzles in English newspapers, but it should keep you guessing for a while.

Worksheet 7

Across

1. Part of the African scene in the children's room (two words)
8. Small, round stones
9. To read out the letters of a word – or a bit of magic
10. The film was so boring – it seemed to go on for ...
11. Describing a powerful, pleasant smell
13. What happens in a story, play, etc. – also a film genre
14. You don't have to take pictures with one of these nowadays – you can use a mobile instead!
17. Semi-precious blue stone
19. Indefinite article before a vowel
20. A zebra might have been part of the lions' ...
22. In cartoons these are often shown as a light bulb coming on in a bubble above someone's head
23. More than just made
25. The African scene in 'The Veldt' could be part of a ... (two words)

Down

1. Opposite to bottom
2. All around you – like the very realistic veldt scene
3. Mr Jones will take your ... now, Madam
4. Make certain
5. People in Britain like to eat one of these – but you can feed it to the chickens, too! (two words)
6. Not done secretly
7. Not wanting to do something
10. Something given out by a source of some kind (music, gas, etc.)
12. People who don't like camping usually stay in ...
15. Source of 10 down
16. One of these might enjoy The Merry Widow Waltzl
18. The lions looked up immediately. They were very much on the ...
21. You can keep small cats as these – but not big ones!
24. Poor parents! At the end of 'The Veldt' they have to ...

Worksheet 7 Solution

1 T	H	2 A	T	3 C	H	4 E	D	5 F	L	6 O	O	7 R
O		M		A		N		I		V		E
8 P	E	B	B	L	E	S		9 S	P	E	L	L
		I		L		U		H		R		U
10 E	V	E	R		11 A	R	O	M	A	T	I	C
M		N		12 H		E		E				T
13 A	C	T	I	O	N		14 C	A	M	15 E	R	A
N				T		16 D		L		M		N
17 A	G	18 A	T	E		19 A	N		D	I	E	T
T		L		L		N		21 P		T		
22 I	D	E	A	S		23 C	R	E	A	T	E	24 D
O		R				E		T		E		I
25 N	A	T	U	R	E	R	E	S	E	R	V	E

Klausur 1

Give a Boy a Gun

Morton Rhue

The following extract is taken from the novel *Give a Boy a Gun* by Morton Rhue. The work of fiction is about a school massacre at Middleton High School, carried out by two students, Gary and Brendan. Large parts of the book focus on their development. Allison Findley is Gary's and Brendan's friend.

You know how sometimes you go to a movie and you come out and for a little while you sort of feel like one of the characters? Maybe you even talk like them? Brendan, Gary, and I went to one of these dumb horror movies. There's a scene where the killer guy picks up one of his victims and throws him off an overpass, right in front of a big truck going underneath.
So, it's night and we were walking home, and Brendan stops on the overpass and watches the cars going by underneath. He just stood there, Gary and I called him to come on, but he wouldn't. We didn't know what he was doing. All of a sudden he starts to throw something. It turned out he wasn't throwing anything, just going through the motion. But it looked like it to us, and to the cars underneath. There's this horrible screeching and squealing of tires and you knew cars were skidding and swerving to get out of the way, and you're sure any second you're going to hear a crash, but it didn't happen, I wanted to run, get out of there before someone came up and caught us. But Brendan wouldn't run.
He just walked up to us with a big smile on his face and said, didn't we think that was the wicked coolest thing?

Allison Findley

From: Morton Rhue: *Give a Boy a Gun*, hg. v. Herbert Geisen, Reclam, Ditzingen 2003, p. 70,

---

[1] **overpass** (Straßen-)Überführung [2] **to go through the motion** (nur) die Bewegung machen [3] **to screech** kreischen **to squeal** quietschen [4] **to skid** rutschen **to swerve** schleudern

Activities

1. **Wat does Brendan do?**
2. **Analyse the way Allison Findley describes what Brendan does. Have a closer look at her choice of words and sentences.**
3. **Do you think that "dumb horror movies" can have a bad impact on young people? Give reasons.**
4. **Even though young people know that horror movies are "dumb" they seem to like them. Why? Give reasons.**

Klausur 1 Solution

1. Brendan stops on the overpass and watches the cars below. Then he pretends to throw something down onto the cars/goes through the motion of throwing something down onto the cars.

2. 'He just stood there' (l. 7) – B. is obviously fascinated by the stream of cars, and is linking the scene with the one in the film.
   'All of a sudden he starts to throw something' (l. 8 f.) – Use of present tense for dramatic effect. At this point the writer allows us to believe he actually is throwing something.
   'It turned out ... motion.' (l. 9 f.) – The reader is told that Brendan didn't actually throw anything – we feel a sense of relief.
   'horrible screeching and squealing/skidding and swerving' (l. 11 f.) – Emotive language and use of alliteration (main lexical items all begin with 's') to convey the dramatic events on the road below.
   'B. wouldn't run ... big smile on his face ... wicked coolest thing' (ll. 14 – 16) – These reactions show that B. has no fear of being caught, on the contrary, this was a marvellous experience for him, which he wants to enjoy/savour for as long as possible.
   We can assume that he would be capable of actually throwing something as in the film.

3. (See the note on the cartoon *You better not;* cartoon on p. 54 of the student's book, note on p. 68 of the teachers' book)

4. Some points which could be made:
   exciting, plenty of action, some (young) people like vicarious thrills/like to have a good scream, may like clinging to partner at scary moments, may like forgetting all about everyday life for the time being

Klausur 2

Moving Images

Daniel Frampton

Media studies is often denigrated[1] as useless. Yet at the same time people complain that we don't know enough about the effects of television and movies on children. We need to understand the "affects" of moving images – how their forms move us directly, emotionally. In a sense we need philosophies of film before we can have sociologies of media. And film images are being investigated not only by theorists and philosophers, but also by artists and film-makers.

In her recent video work, *Family History*, Gillian Wearing recreates an afternoon-talk-show set, and forces open its nature as a brightly coloured "idealised home". Daytime TV looks as though it has been designed by seasonal affective disorder[2] researchers, with bright lights and colourful furnishings that create a feeling of cheeriness. Daytime soaps also come with their own bright ontology[3] about life and relationships, with camera movements that relax us and close-ups that make us think we are getting a direct access to emotions, creating a kind of false engagement.

So how do we combat this menace[4] in our living rooms? If kids are mentally soaked by the moving image, and by its frequent changes of form, they need a concept of film that gives them a critical mode of attention towards these forms. Showing them how films "think" about their characters and spaces (using framing, movement, editing) could be a first step. They can then apply this to the media that surround them. They might then recognise and resist the propaganda of exploitative visual media (overbranded[5] pop videos, seductive advertising, the visual hypnotism of late-night cash-quiz shows).

Traditional film-makers are also revealing the constructed nature of cinema films. The opening shot of Michael Haneke's *Hidden* looks like a bland establishing shot, but is then revealed as the point of view of an unseen observer – and in this movement from omniscience to subjectivity the film helps us understand how all images are created: that media images hide as much truth as they reveal.

But the thinking of film can be also be creative and beautiful. In the opening image of *The Constant Gardener*, the film does something strange. Justin is saying goodbye to Tessa in an aircraft hangar, and the film keeps them in half-darkness, with a bright runway and plane in the background. As she leaves him and moves outside, the film increases the light and softens the scene so that she and the plane become a blur, with Justin still clearly defined in the foreground, watching her disappear, almost literally. In this moment of film-thinking we seem to receive an understanding of the relationship between Justin and Tessa – we feel a certain divorce between them.

Film seems to be thinking right in front of us. [...] The point is that both the daytime chatshow and the video news report also involve this choice, this belief about what they show [...]. If we begin to understand how film "thinks" we will start to understand how moving images affect our life and being.

---

[1] **to denigrate** to say things to make sb or sth seem less important [2] **seasonal affective disorder** an illness that makes sb feel sad in winter [3] **ontology** philosophical studies about the nature of existence [4] **menace** sth dangerous [5] **overbranded** containing too many brand names

As the Hungarian film theorist Bela Balazs wrote back in 1945: "We must be better connoisseurs of the film if we are not to be as much at the mercy of perhaps the greatest intellectual and spiritual influence of our age as to some blind and irresistible elemental force."

Daniel Frampton: "Moving Images", in: *The Guardian*, October 23, 2006, p. 30

Activities

1. **Why and how should we get a "better understanding of how film and television affect us emotionally"?**
2. **Examine why and how Daniel Frampton includes the readers.**
3. **Following Daniel Frampton, "we need to understand the 'affects' of moving images – how their forms move us directly, emotionally." Do you agree with his view? Give reasons.**
4. **Write a letter to the editor reacting to Daniel Frampton's claims.**

Klausur 2 Solution

1. If we understand how film and television affect us emotionally, we will be better able to resist attempts to manipulate us. This could be done by explaining film techniques such as framing, moving, editing etc., and then applying these findings to examples of exploitative media.

2. By the frequent use of 'we' and 'us' throughout the article, for example. Students should quote some other typical examples.

3. – moving images are potentially very powerful – may therefore evoke very powerful/dangerous/uncontrolled reactions in an unprepared viewer
   – a viewer who knows that he is being manipulated, and understands the mechanisms involved, will be able to maintain some distance from the images on the screen/avoid being totally involved and therefore extremely vulnerable to advertising/other forms of propaganda/emotional exploitation

4. Some useful expressions:

   Sir,
   I read Daniel Frampton's article in *The Guardian* of October 23 with great interest.
   As a teenager myself, I am well aware ...
   I'm sure we are manipulated in various ways, for example ...
   I think it would be very helpful if ...
   I had not realised ...
   I found the analysis of scenes from films ...
   I don't really feel 'at the mercy' of the media, but ...
   At my school ...
   I will certainly try ... in future.
   Yours sincerely,

Discover ...

Shakespeare-Textausgaben
Landeskundliche Themenhefte

Herausgegeben von
Klaus Hinz und Engelbert Thaler (ab 2007)

Aspects of the English Language
Von Ralf Weskamp
62 S. Best.-Nr. **978-3-14-040045-9**
Lehrerheft. Best.-Nr. **978-3-14-040065-7**

The Mass Media – From Gutenberg to Gates
Von Stephen Speight und Karsten Witsch
64 S. Best.-Nr. **978-3-14-040088-6**
Lehrerheft. Best.-Nr. **978-3-14-040096-1**

The Different Faces of Britain
Von Stephen Speight
64 S. Best.-Nr. **978-3-14-040085-5**
Lehrerheft. Best.-Nr. **978-3-14-040095-4**

Our Environment – A State of Emergency?
Von Stephen Speight
59 S. Best.-Nr. **978-3-14-040108-1**
Lehrerheft. Best.-Nr. **978-3-14-040109-8**

Hispanics in America
Von Veronika Kaiser und James Martin
72 S. Best.-Nr. **978-3-14-040044-2**
Lehrerheft. Best.-Nr. **978-3-14-040064-0**

The American Dream – Inventing a Nation
Von Hanspeter Bauer
74 S. Best.-Nr. **978-3-14-040086-2**
Lehrerheft. Best.-Nr. **978-3-14-040087-9**

The American South
Von Jürgen Einhoff und Katharina Einhoff
72 S. Best.-Nr. **978-3-14-040052-7**
Lehrerheft. Best.-Nr. **978-3-14-040076-3**

British and American Youth Culture
Von Hannspeter Bauer und Gudrun Vesper
64 S. Best.-Nr. **978-3-14-040053-4**
Lehrerheft. Best.-Nr. **978-3-14-040077-0**

Ireland – Changes and Challenges
Von Maria Eisenmann
55 S. Best.-Nr. **978-3-14-040110-4**
Lehrerheft. Best.-Nr. **978-3-14-040111-1**

The Australian Aboriginals
Von Elsa Zettelmann-Kunde
70 S. Best.-Nr. **978-3-14-040042-8**
Lehrerheft. Best.-Nr. **978-3-14-040062-6**

Canada – More than Mounties and Lumberjacks
Von Martin Kohn
56 S. Best.-Nr. **978-3-14-040082-4**
Lehrerheft. Best.-Nr. **978-3-14-040092-3**

Africa – Postcolonial Experiences
Von Monika Teichmann
70 S. Best.-Nr. **978-3-14-040100-5**
Lehrerheft. Best.-Nr. **978-3-14-040101-2**

India – Tradition and Transformation
Von Michaela Banzhaf und Alexandra Peschel
51 S. Best.-Nr. **978-3-14-040098-5**
Lehrerheft. Best.-Nr. **978-3-14-040099-2**

Distant Neighbours. Projects in Intercultural Learning
Von Anja Beuter, Peter Dieckow und Karl Heinz Wagner
67 S. Best.-Nr. **978-3-14-040049-7**
Lehrerheft. Best.-Nr. **978-3-14-040071-8**

Globalisation – Blessing or Curse?
Von Jürgen Einhoff, Klaus Hinz und Karl Heinz Wagner
68 S. Best.-Nr. **978-3-14-040059-6**
Lehrerheft. Best.-Nr. **978-3-14-040089-3**

The Fascination and Risks of Technology
Von Stephen Speight
56 S. Best.-Nr. **978-3-14-040055-8**
Lehrerheft. Best.-Nr. **978-3-14-040079-4**

William Shakespeare: Macbeth
Von Rainer Gocke und Angela Stock
136 S. Best.-Nr. **978-3-14-040041-1**
Lehrerheft. Best.-Nr. **978-3-14-040061-9**

William Shakespeare: Othello
Von Anke Weber
147 S. Best.-Nr. **978-3-14-040069-5**
Lehrerheft. Best.-Nr. **978-3-14-040102-9**

William Shakespeare: Romeo and Juliet
Von Norbert Timm
143 S. Best.-Nr. **978-3-14-040056-5**
Lehrerheft. Best.-Nr. **978-3-14-040081-7**

William Shakespeare: Bits From The Bard
Nach Themenschwerpunkten zusammengestellt
Von Norbert Timm
48 S. Best.-Nr. **978-3-14-040057-2**
Lehrerheft. Best.-Nr. **978-3-14-040097-8**

William Shakespeare: A Midsummer Night's Dream
Von Rainer Gocke und Angela Stock
104 S. Best.-Nr. **978-3-14-040058-9**
Lehrerheft. Best.-Nr. **978-3-14-040068-8**

Weitere Titel sind in Vorbereitung.

Schöningh Verlag
Postfach 2540
33055 Paderborn

Schöningh

Fordern Sie unseren Prospekt zur kompletten Reihe an:
Informationen 0800 / 18 18 787 (freecall)
info@schoeningh.de / www.schoeningh-schulbuch.de